LIFE AT THE EDGE

by

Jan Greenman

Living with ADHD and Aspergers Syndrome

The true story of Luke's life with labels

Published by Jan Greenman

Published by Jan Greenman

18 The Parklands

Hullavington

Wiltshire

ISBN 978-0-9554982-0-6

A catalogue record for this book is available from the British Library

Front Cover photo by kind permission of Anna Durrant
www.durrant1.plus.com

Printed by
Antony Rowe Ltd,
Bumper's Farm, Chippenham
Wiltshire SN14 6LH

01249 659705

> Start a child in the way he should go, and when he
> is old he will not turn from it.
>
> **Proverbs 22 v 6**

CONTENTS

ACKNOWLEDGEMENTS

I would like to thank the following people, in the random order in which my brain thinks of them, without whom my life would be a different story and this book would never have been written: -

Luke, my uniquely remarkable boy, without whom there would be no book. You have rewritten every preconception that I had about parenting, about life itself. I am so proud of you and no, I'm not paying you for the privilege of being your mum

Abbi, my feisty little poppet, so gentle by nature, who has the wisest head on her very petite shoulders and without whom I would never have coped and that is the truth

Libbi, who has been my fiercest protector even when she couldn't bear to see my pain

My Mum, who has listened and listened when there was nothing else to do and **My Dad,** who let her!

Cathy, who taught me that dreams are sometimes all we have between us and the next failure

Trev, alias Nick Corless. He knows who he is and he is in the next book

Ann Baker, Lisa's mum who is one brave lady.

Fran and Maggie, who love others much and themselves least

James Gray, who championed Luke long before 'reality anything' became fashionable

Nigel Mansell, who is a very worthy hero for any boy to aspire to

Auntie Kath and Auntie Tubers, you have been loyal, loving and very kind. Kindness is everything when you are at the end of your emotional tether

Elliott, thank you for being a friend to Luke all those years ago. Who could ever have predicted how it would all turn out? Life is stranger than fiction Babes!

Tim and Wendy, you are very special people and you know why

Elaine, our friendship is God-given, you inspire my faith

Heidi, you are one of life's encouragers and that is a rare gift in anyone, let alone someone so young. I love you, please have some fun!

David B. - we will remember you long after the cancer has claimed you. Thankyou for the raw honesty, based on circumstance, that your friendship brings us.

Jane and Peter, our new neighbours who trust us to feed their cats and showed such understanding

Auntie Joyce and Uncle Alan, who live in Australia and whose enthusiasm and zest for life has always been inspirational

Johnny Francis, to whom I owe a huge Thank you. Without my very kind-hearted 'obedient servant' I would have admitted defeat a long time ago

Lastly but in every way not least, **VHG** who has taught me the art of multi-tasking with infinite patience and, more potently, about the real meaning of true love which gives and gives and expects nothing in return

INTRODUCTION - LIFE AT THE EDGE

This book is the true story of a boy called Luke. It is his story, but because we are his family, it is our story too.

Luke wants his story told, he wants people to understand him and others like him and he knows that knowledge is the key to life.

Luke has so many labels that he has his own business cards printed with all the letters after his name 'Luke Dicker: - child with Aspergers Syndrome, ADHD and chronic anxiety' which he hands out to introduce himself. Like a lot of children on the autistic spectrum he is hell on two legs: - funny, angry, aggressive, misogynistic, politically incorrect, pedantic and very insightful into his own condition. He is a toddler emotionally, with the intellect of a twenty year-old all wrapped up in a teenager's body. He can bore the pants off you or fascinate you by equal measures in a loud and monotone voice but you can't ignore or forget him. Black or white, no grey areas. He takes everything literally and personally.

Our MP James Gray is a friend, courtesy of Luke. He took Luke on a guided tour of the House of Lords, House of Commons and even onto the roof of the House of Commons to hear Big Ben strike 11am. A very important fact. Luke likes facts. Facts make sense of things. Our GP has contributed to this book and I wish I had read it years ago. It is both factual and anecdotal, covering education, or more specifically the lack of specialist education in our county of Wiltshire and our subsequent ongoing fight to obtain it, medical issues of Luke's early years, including MMR, *Ritalin* and its' effect from both mine and Luke's perception, his obsessions and habits, language, relationships, his behaviour and what drives it, sensory sensitivities, disability allowance and how to apply and also his sister Abbi's role in our family as a young carer, plus the exposed truth of our family life.

Every aspect of Luke's behaviour is unwrapped in terms that both professionals and parents alike will find helpful. His labels came slowly, separately and sadly, in many ways too late. Certainly too late to save my marriage. So many children are currently being diagnosed on the autistic spectrum that every person associated with the child, from parents to

viii

teachers to grandparents, needs to read a book like this to understand all the 'Lukes' out there. Most importantly it helps parents to know that they are not alone and that their child does have a voice. I have included tips from myself, Luke and Abbi and I am passionate about changing people's perception of, and particularly the judgment that comes with the behaviour associated with autism. Even with all the information available on autistic spectrum disorders, at grass roots level it is still a real fight to get any kind of help, understanding and most importantly, (certainly in our experience) specialist education for our children, in this the 21st century! It appears to be a question of resources.

In my life before Luke I was the Treasurer of a private merchant bank, headhunted by them and my appointment approved by the Bank of England. I have not been able to return to work since his birth. He is a full-time occupation.

Luke is more than happy to see his name in print. He is articulate and insightful into his condition and wants to speak for himself and others like him. Of course, being a Dicker, (which is actually a verb meaning to barter) he would like to be paid for his voice. Trust him to be named, literally, the way he takes everything. He negotiates everything. Everything has a price, even behaviour. Negotiating is one of his many obsessions.

The title of this book is **'Life at The Edge'**. **'The Edge'** was the name of our family house where we lived until our marriage finally fell apart last year. It proved to be prophetically accurate!

There are many reasons why Luke's story needs to be told, not least because he is a very brave boy who leaves the safety of his house to venture into a world so alien, and sometimes, so scary that it takes a huge amount of courage just to open his eyes each morning and face another day.

Some days he can't do that. He can't tear himself from sleep to the familiar gut-wrenching fear of another day. Other days the fear makes him cry, then vomit with anxiety.

The fear is a relatively new thing. It has come with growing up. Aged ten years to be precise. Luke likes precise detail. Facts are safe and he can quote them at you until you beg him to stop. He then gets upset because he is sharing his knowledge with you. That is a good thing, isn't it? Before the fear came, Luke was like a human whirlwind of activity. Most of it frantic, some of it dangerous and some destructive. Bursts of creative genius would spring out of nowhere and disappear just as quickly, leaving us wondering whether we had imagined it. One day when he was eight years old, Luke took some pastel crayons, a piece of paper and his mind and set to work in a cloud of pastel dust. Within a few minutes he had drawn a pelican, a really beautiful pelican. He did it for his grandfather. The fact that he had such detail stored in his mind and was able to recreate it in minutes with pastels was amazing. My friend Cathy is an artist, a sculptor and she loved it. Yet he never repeated that picture. When I asked him to draw one for me, he explained that he couldn't. The picture wasn't held in his mind for me but for his grandfather. And now the memory of it had gone from his head and onto the paper.

I am Luke's mum and there are days, many days, when I want to resign. Please don't misunderstand me. I love Luke with a passion. I love Luke more than even I know but I live with Luke and I am the bottom line. When my line goes wobbly, who straightens me out? That is another reason for writing this book. Although we live in an amazing world of high technology, of achievements, of progress and of change, we all shut our doors and live our lives. Loneliness is just a front door away.

Well, life behind our front door is a bit of a nightmare and although to speak of it seems like a betrayal of my boy, if you are ever to understand then I have to tell it like it is.

JAMES GRAY MP

HOUSE OF COMMONS

LONDON SW1A 0AA

Luke Dicker is an extraordinary boy by any standards, and I very much welcome the publication of this book about his abilities, and the very real difficulties associated with his Asperger's Syndrome.

Too little is known about the various parts of the Autistic Spectrum, and too few outsiders understand the trials and tribulations as well as the blessings of living with someone like Luke.

I hope that this frank and fascinating account of his life and his family's will help other autism sufferers and their carers. More important even than that, I hope that it will help society at large achieve a wider understanding of Aspergers Syndrome, and perhaps help promote a deeper sympathy for those suffering from it.

I salute Luke's openness and the courage and determination of his Mother and Sister, and hope that you greatly enjoy reading their story.

James Gray

xi

CHAPTER 1   A VERY GOOD PLACE TO START. THE BEGINNING

Nothing prepares you for the reality of motherhood. For that moment when you fulfill the purpose for which, as a woman, your body was created.

I was the Treasurer of a private Merchant Bank based in Bristol and my husband Paul had his own courier company based in Swindon. Luke was conceived on a riotous skiing holiday in Verbier, Switzerland with our friends Geoff and Wendy and a big crowd of their friends. Wendy has been an 'inner circle' friend ever since we first met. You need those kinds of friends, the ones who knew you before you had children. They know that you are still you and they bring you back to baseline sometimes. She always makes me laugh, no matter how stressed I am and we always pick up where we left off, no matter if we haven't seen each other for ages. We live too far apart though and I miss her face.

I loved being pregnant. Loved getting fat with good reason. I had 'happy hormones' and didn't have even one day's morning sickness. I worked until three weeks before Luke was due to be born and was planning on returning to work after about three months, all things being equal!

Luke was born on the 6th December 1991, his due date. My labour started 36 hours before and didn't really go to plan. (That's an understatement!) It kept stopping and starting and it was a long, lonely time. Luke's dad had all but passed out at the antenatal classes so we should have guessed that he would feel too unwell to remain in the delivery suite. I had believed in the romantic ideal of birth as presented to women of my liberated generation. The one where you chose when to have your baby and your method of delivery, you played soft music, your partner held your hand and out popped the baby, all nice and clean and controlled, according to your birth plan. We were young professionals and our lives went to plan. Well, everything except anything to do with Luke. (Consequently when I delivered Abbi, our second child, I took a reality pill and my sister Libbi was there, instinctively helping me, woman to woman and the experience was so different.) Knowing Luke now, I am so NOT surprised at how he disrupted everything and yet still managed to arrive on the precise day he was expected at almost mid-day!

Luke is my first-born child and any mum will remember that moment when you meet your first child for the first time. It redefines you as a woman. There is no going back from that moment. The love of a mother is the strongest and most primitive form of love. It asks nothing in return initially and is totally unconditional. That is so much the love that Luke still needs, *demands* from me, that 'baby' love which gives and gives, not expecting anything back. That way, anything I do get is a bonus! He was, to me, the most beautiful baby. 8lbs 7ozs of strapping baby boy, mop of black hair, blue eyes and a very misshapen head from being unceremoniously yanked out, with considerable force, by a suction plunger to the head. Called a ventouse delivery but looking and feeling more like a mediaeval form of torture, it was absolutely the scariest moment of my life, up to that point, when I realised that Luke was in distress and needed to be delivered straight away. Welcome to parenthood, Luke style.

Stitching me up afterwards went on forever and felt like a tapestry in motion. Luke fed as regularly as clockwork, every four hours almost to the minute, right from birth. He had this inbuilt clock that seemed amazing, even then! Getting up in the middle of the night was actually a lovely experience. I remember sitting, (with difficulty - given the tapestry) holding Luke long after he had finished feeding, just for the smell of him in my nostrils. That sweet baby smell that emanates from a baby's head and is so subtly powerful to a mother's protective instincts. Did you know that when you hold your baby in your arms, you automatically pat their bottom in time with your own heartbeat? That, of course, is so familiar to them. For the last few weeks of pregnancy their bum and your heart were fairly closely connected, assuming they weren't in the breach position.

So there were now three of us. Paul, me – Jan, Luke's mum and Luke. Abbi was also conceived on holiday, this time in St. Lucia in the Caribbean. She arrived two years and three months later than Luke and was God's balancing act in our family. Imagine a seesaw. Our family with one child called Luke was always Jan and Luke on one end of the seesaw and Paul on the other. So Luke and I never left the floor. When Abbi came, she was so peaceful, so sweet, and so easy by *comparison,* that she could join Paul's end of the seesaw and our end, mine and Luke's, finally left the ground. That isn't to say that Paul doesn't love Luke, but he certainly wasn't the peaceful, easy option that Abbi was and there are some things that only a mother's love can cope with.

Before Luke was born Paul and I led such busy lives that we didn't actually spend a great deal of time together. For two years I had commuted daily from Bristol to the City of London, a five hour round trip, in my capacity as a money dealer for *Tyndall & Co Ltd.*, a private bank. It was exciting, exhausting and all consuming. I was one of a handful of women in a man's world and it was lovely. I was treated with respect once I had proved myself, which meant ignoring the dirty jokes, swearing and irreverent attitude to just about every tragedy and I found that my femininity worked for me, hugely. Then I had been headhunted for the Treasurer's position in Bristol. Paul was working out of Swindon, so we were like ships that passed each other in the night and it suited us fine. Looking back now, we lived a very privileged yet superficial life in many respects. We worked hard, played hard and didn't even scratch the surface of a real relationship. (One day our Chief executive gave me a £10,000 bonus and I moaned about having to give the tax man £4,000 of it!)

Jan's tip: Can I just talk about comparisons for a moment. Most people hate comparisons and I do in some respects because we are all individuals, but when your child is a Luke you need to compare. Otherwise you never know what is normal, what you can and should expect of your child's behaviour, what you need to try and modify and what you just have to accept. Normal is another taboo word but it's a yardstick and we need one of those in our house. Luke would love to be normal, even though he doesn't know what that would feel like. It doesn't stop him dreaming of being normal though and there are days when I tell him that I wish he was normal, he understands why I say that and he doesn't hold it against me, although I hold it against myself.

Luke's tip: Don't get hung up on words. (He loves formal language and uses pedantic and overbearing words at times and yet he can swear like an English football fan, or more to the point, Billy Connolly, Scottish accent and all. None of the words he uses are meant to cause offence but they inevitably do. He would very much like you to see beyond the words to the boy using them.) Please and Thank you. Throw in lots of polite ones too for good measure, because if you are polite, people seem to like you better.

CHAPTER 2 THE NIGHTMARE BEGINS

At seven weeks old, Luke suddenly went very floppy and pale one Thursday evening. Until then he had been a textbook baby, feeding every four hours as regular as clockwork, sleeping in between and very alert when awake. He looked at me so intently; almost as though he knew what I was thinking and I loved him utterly. The worst part of parenting this far in had been feeding him. He latched on to my nipple and sucked with a vice-like grip. The mid-wife was so impressed with my resolve to carry on feeding, despite my torn and bleeding nipples, that she told everyone who would listen about my bravery! Who wants to be famous for their tattered nipples?

I sat up all night with Luke, not wanting to make a drama out of a crisis and he seemed to recover. In the morning I called our GP and she visited at the end of surgery. She said that Luke had some sort of virus and he did have a rash developing down one side of his face. If he went floppy again over the weekend I was to call the emergency doctor.

On the Sunday he was quiet and suddenly went floppy and was very pale to the point of deathly white. We called the emergency doctor as instructed and so began the end of safety, normality, reason. Luke was admitted to hospital straight away and we heard every parent's nightmare word, Meningitis. Luke was taken from me and immediately given a lumbar puncture. My protective instincts went into overdrive and I felt like kicking the doctor who was putting this whacking great needle into his little spine with no obvious finesse or gentleness, just a palpable sense of urgency. Normally this procedure would be done under anaesthetic as it is so painful, but time is of the essence in the diagnosis of the bacterial form of meningitis, so it was immediate and made him scream with shock and pain. The agonies of hearing him scream, of not being able to hold him, comfort him, ripped me apart. Every parent whose child is sick knows that agony. It is so shocking when it happens to you. So starkly shocking when your safe, cosy world is suddenly and brutally ripped apart with no warning. Illness - menacing, cold and no respecter of persons had come knocking on our door and how I longed, still do, for the innocence of the days before that Sunday. You never know what you have until you don't have it any more, which is why every day should be treated, in some measure, as a treasured gift.

I have often wondered what Luke remembers, deep in his brain, of the ensuing weeks. Certainly what happened next changed me forever. Carefree days became a thing of the past, and to a great extent that is still true. I suppose that is parenthood in a word for me - *Worry*, deep, deep down worry that I have learnt to live with, got no choice on that one, but it is ever present and ever draining. I've got the lines on my forehead to prove my words and I've earned every one.

We entered the goldfish-bowl world of hospital life. Luke did not have the bacterial form of meningitis. He was diagnosed with encephalitis, a virus affecting the brain, which made him deeply unconscious for periods of time and he was a very sick little baby. There was no treatment and the biggest worry of all was that during his periods of unconsciousness, it was difficult to tell if he was breathing. His lips would go blue, his face grey and he was floppy to the point of no muscle tone. We were taught to resuscitate him but I couldn't do it. When he had to have a general anaesthetic for a brain scan I ran out of the room, I just couldn't stand by and watch his vulnerability and it was Paul who hated needles, hospitals, the whole caboodle, who stayed with his unconscious little body as they put him inside the scanner and started taking pictures of his brain. Luke had so many tests, including being starved for 24 hours - which was like a form of torture for both of us, because he was screaming for food and my milk was spurting out in response to his screams. Again I had to walk away and leave him, going against every maternal instinct in my body and brain.

Every day in hospital felt like a week and life became an unreal zone, a zombie zone where you went through the motions and looked the same but nothing was the same and normal life was fantasyland. It is interesting just how much a person can cope with and rise above, when you have to. I wondered if it is the same in every country or is it true that the British do cope better with a crisis? (That stiff upper lip mentality that took us through two world wars with not a counsellor in sight and an incredible spirit of shared survival.)

Later, when we were allowed to take Luke home for periods of time and he suddenly had 'an episode', as his Consultant Dr. Tim Chambers used to call them, (for want of a better expression) I would dial 999 and wait for an ambulance crew to arrive and administer oxygen etc. before returning us to the safety of the hospital. That flashing blue light and loud siren approaching has never looked more welcome. Can anyone explain to me why I was too terrified to give Luke mouth to mouth? If it was your child I wouldn't hesitate, but I just couldn't cope with the reality of what was happening to my baby. I had been responsible for a money book of £380million in the bank and had taken that in my stride but I couldn't take the responsibility of my child's life in my hands. I tortured myself with the 'what if' scenarios long after the danger was past each time, but every time it happened I quietly went to pieces, much to my shame.

Eventually, Dr Chambers decided to refer Luke to the Royal Brompton Hospital in London to see Professor David Southall and try to discover exactly what was happening to him during the recurring episodes of unconsciousness. By now I was so utterly desperate with worry that I was begging the hospital to monitor Luke around the clock to try and discover what was happening to him. My nerves were absolutely shattered and I just didn't know how to cope with the awful fear that consumed me each time he fell into that deep state of unconsciousness. The hospital discharged him as soon as possible, once he had recovered sufficiently, because bed space was at a premium. On the one hand that was fantastic because I always *wanted* to believe that this time would be the last time, but bitter experience said that it wasn't and I just couldn't handle it any more.

By this time Luke had been in and out of Southmead Hospital in Bristol for over three months, more in than out, and we had watched several very sick children being admitted, treated and then leave, well again. We saw several babies come in with the meningicoccal form of meningitis, watched the horrible septicemia rash spreading across their little bodies as doctors chased veins up their systems trying to get the life saving antibiotics directly into the blood stream before their veins shut down. One little girl had the antibiotics put into the only vein still accessible right on the top of her head. It was awesome, seeing the responsibility on those junior doctors, some of whom had been on duty for the longest time.

A neurologist in Bristol had diagnosed Luke's recent episodes as a form of epilepsy and started him on medication, *Carbamazepine* or *Tegratol* to use its' more common name. However, the episodes didn't stop and we asked for Luke to come off the medication as he had developed an open, weeping sore on his neck that wouldn't heal. The neurologist refused to withdraw medication, preferring instead to increase the dose in a bid to try and control Luke's episodes. However, this still had no effect and so bravely, and against medical advice, we asked to stop the medication. We had been told that there was no precedent for giving a baby of Luke's age a drug of that kind and so side effects were undocumented. On that basis it seemed sensible to stop medication if it wasn't working. The neurologist recommended a controlled withdrawal after two years but for me the stakes were too high. It seemed crazy to keep giving him a drug that wasn't working and had potentially serious side effects to his developing brain. We stopped the drug over the course of a week and learnt something about doctors in the process. They like text book cases and if you don't fit into that category then they put you at arm's length because they don't know what else to do with you. It's nothing personal but it sure feels like it. We also learnt that the brain is an unknown quantity, even for the experts. That was so scary. Having to make such big decisions against medical advice seemed the wrong way round but all I can say is that instinct is God-given for a reason. I have had to rely on mine over the ensuing years; there's been nothing else on offer a lot of the time. Even as a new mum that instinct was very strong. Luke's smell was different when he was about to have an episode and I sensed that instinctively, I knew if I was holding him that he was about to flake out just from the smell of his head. The soft spot on his head used to bulge and pulse too.

And so it was that Paul and I found ourselves following an ambulance up the M4 from Bristol to London. We weren't allowed to travel with Luke and I must say that was his first proper journey of more than a few miles and his first proper bout of travel sickness, from which he has suffered ever since. So, looking on the positive side, it is probably the only time I haven't had to clear up after him!

It felt totally surreal, following this ambulance with two nurses, two ambulance crew and one baby all the way to London. We had gone from the extreme of self-reliance in our respective careers to the despair of having absolutely no control over our life, emotions and circumstances. The nurses in Bristol had become our friends and they were very good at making our new reality an easier one to accept as they were so matter of factly professional, yet kind and reasoned too. They became like family and their attitude to us became all-important. There was one very brusque nurse though, who was usually dismissive and sometimes downright rude and she held enormous power over me, reducing me to tears frequently in my vulnerable state.

At this time Paul and I were a team. We were both frightened and out of our depth and so we clung to each other, the only two people who knew what it felt like to be in our position, hoping and praying that things would get better. It is amazing how you pray when a crisis comes that close.

We were given a parents' room in the Royal Brompton and met Professor Southall, an expert on unusual childhood conditions and cot deaths, amongst other things. (I read an article in the Daily Mail recently that said he is an expert on proving Munchausens Syndrome by proxy against the parents of children who presented very similar symptoms to Luke.) He has also been involved in the case of Sally Clark, the solicitor who was wrongly convicted of killing her babies on the incorrect statistical evidence of Dr Roy Meadows. Medical experts have a strong voice so they should use it discriminately, particularly against a mother, who only in very, very rare cases has anything but her child's best interests at heart. It says something about those people who are evangelically determined to prove that a mother is capable of the worst thing a mother could be accused of. Hurting her own child. How have they been given that amount of power by law which allowed them to make such an assumption and then set out to prove it by quoting unreal statistics or their own opinion, based on their medical reputation and with no other hard evidence?

We would have been referred to Dr Peter Fleming, the expert on cot death who had discovered that putting a baby to sleep on its' back was much safer. When Ann Diamond's baby Sebastian died she met Dr Fleming and his research in New Zealand formed a major part of her subsequent campaign. However, by some strange irony at that time, Dr Fleming had a Bell's palsy of the face and was being treated with the identical drug, *Tegratol,* to Luke. So we were sent to London instead. Shame because I always wanted to meet Dr. Fleming. His reputation locally was of the highest.

We also met other parents whose babies had very similar symptoms to Luke's. Professor Southall wired Luke up to various machines that monitored his vital signs, including E.E.G., E.C.G., and transcutaneous skin oxygen levels and recorded 'an event' on a little memory card when one occurred so that he could see exactly what was happening. I was taught to recalibrate the machinery and re-site it every four hours, even through the night, so it didn't burn Luke's skin. This in itself was terrifying to someone like me who is a real technophobe. I hate machines and it was quite a complicated procedure but the motivation was the highest and so I learnt very quickly. I had to. After a week's stay we were sent home. Life had gone from managing a bank's balance sheet, with all the associated socializing that goes with the territory, to sitting in one room with a sick baby wired up to a power point. Even taking a shower was a luxury. I thought I knew what stress was at work, but what I hadn't appreciated was that most of it was positive stress with solutions, responses and rewards attached and a social life to match. This level of emotional stress was beyond numbness. The only thing that kept us going was Luke and yet he was the cause of the problem! That has been true ever since and is the paradox of life with Luke.

To take Luke anywhere meant using a power pack with a limited life and it was easier and safer to stay put. I think it took me about two years to get used to just leaving the house again without feeling terrified and even now I like to go prepared for any eventuality! It makes packing for holidays a nightmare but I am usually proved right! Our only outings were to the neurological ward of the local mental hospital (that was an awfully depressing experience) to read Luke's data and to the hospital to see Dr Chambers, Luke's Consultant, who said to me during one visit that when he died, they would cut him open and engraved on his heart would be the words LUKE DICKER. He was very puzzled by Luke as, even with all his monitoring, there were no clear answers as to what was happening to him and at one time he thought that Luke might be suffering from something called Ondine's curse, a very rare and potentially fatal illness where the patient who falls asleep stops breathing and dies. Once it has been diagnosed however, it is relatively easy to treat. (Actually, professionally speaking, I think he hoped that Luke did have it, because that would have made him well known in medical circles overnight, due to the rarity of the condition.)

My bank were fantastic during this time, holding my position open and letting me keep my company car for over a year with no prospect of returning to work. In fact I have never worked since, for money that is!

Jan's tip: Don't be afraid to rely on your instinct for your child. And please, doctors and other professionals who deal with us and our children, listen to us. We do know our children. We live with them and we deserve your respect. We feel at our most vulnerable when our children are sick and we need looking after too. Being held at arm's length is so patronising, frightening even and we need every reassurance.

Luke's tip: Don't patronise me. I am at least as smart as you, if twice as ugly, so to speak. Please treat me like your equal. I have a sense that knows when someone doesn't like me, or is patronising me and I am very good at sussing people's motives out. I can be quite cold blooded, because I don't really feel the way you do. People may see me as manipulative but it is the way my brain works. It tries to find the advantage for me in every situation because otherwise I am at a disadvantage. That is my motive and my motive is not the same as someone whose brain thinks in an emotional way. I like facts and so I weigh up the facts that I know about a person. For example: my mum's weak points are that she hates being called fat, she likes spending money and she is very sensitive to criticism about being my mum because people who don't understand us, which is most of the population, think she is too kind. They think she can change my behaviour by being fierce but I am programmed to think the way I think. I don't try to change the way you think but I do have to try and understand how you think because you are the lucky ones. You think in the way that society is programmed to behave. So I have to use my intelligence because I can't rely on feelings that I don't have.

If I am mad with my mum, I attack her with words and she usually falls for it, which means that I have won the argument. This is also dangerous knowledge to share with you because now she knows and so I have lost my advantage. For me, winning is my motivation for doing something. The only way I know what is what is to compare. I relate better to the animal kingdom than other humans so I used to ask my mum "who is the strongest, a lion or a shark?" She used to say she didn't know because they lived in different environments so then I used to ask, "which one do you think?" I have to do this as my reference point for everything, although obviously my questions are more grown up now. Nothing about life makes much sense to me and I managed to get most things wrong until I was older and could use my own reasoning for trying to control how I behave, even if I don't know why it works that way. It is the way that it is done and I have to try and fit in. My friend Gabe told me the other day that I fit in sometimes but even when I don't and I am really annoying, life is still more interesting with me around. Is that what you call a compliment?

CHAPTER 3 GOING FOR BROKE

At about six months old, after spending a great deal of that time in hospital, Luke began to stop having his 'episodes'. He never did have a fit in the classic way; he lost consciousness, went grey and appeared to be dead. It was never clear whether he did stop breathing altogether but the ambulance crews used to give him oxygen and this did seem to revive him. His monitors showed that his oxygen levels would drop rapidly and dramatically and his breathing would rattle in his little throat before seeming to stop. It was impossible to pick up a pulse sometimes. One day, my birthday actually, my Auntie Kath was visiting him in the hospital. (I can remember my birthdays by Luke's dramas.) She is a nursing sister tutor who ran the *Elizabeth Backwell* hospital in Clifton, Bristol and was holding him when he passed out. She admitted to me later that she had never been so scared as she could feel his pulse fluttering, then fading away. Actually, in a funny kind of way, that was reassuring to me because if she was scared, as a professional nurse, then my panic as his mum was more measurable.

Whilst in hospital, Luke's three-month triple vaccination became due. His consultant advised us to 'go for broke' and have it. He wasn't sure what effect it would have on Luke but felt that it was better for him to have it than not. Dr Chambers was a big man who seemed god-like when he did his rounds. Everyone treated him deferentially and it would have taken a brave person to cross him! He inspired confidence so we took his advice and Luke had his first jab. He immediately lost consciousness and did his usual dramatic disappearing act, although this time he was in hospital and the staff sprang into action. I remember just sitting there like a zombie, too utterly exhausted to move, relieved that this time I didn't have to call an ambulance and take another blue light ride, praying that he would be ok. The awful fear was always there that *this time* he wouldn't be revived and the terror used to paralyse me. I sat there, apparently oblivious to the situation, until he was brought back to the land of the living. Then I would cry quiet tears of relief. (I have always loved the Italian way of reacting, dramatic, hands flying, accompanied by much noise and loud sobbing. Probably because it is so opposite to my 'buttoned-up' coping mechanism - the result of a repressed childhood!)

After the immediate drama was over and Luke was brought back to consciousness, the localised site of the jab started to swell. It became red and angry, the size of a small fist. To this day Luke still has a hole in his thigh where the needle went in, about the size of a one pence piece.

This convinced us that he shouldn't have any further vaccinations. Consequently he did not have the controversial MMR vaccination. We are so pleased that we made that choice for him, as from present evidence, there are a group of children who are vulnerable to the triple vaccine and Luke would fall into that category. He may well have developed extreme autism as a result. It wasn't an easy decision to make because there was, still is, a lot of pressure to conform to the Government's programme. We were given dire warnings of what would happen if Luke wasn't vaccinated but no assurances of safety if he was. There was a strange sense of being asked to take a gamble and that is not acceptable when the stakes are so high, i.e. your child's health. We wanted to make an informed choice and we weren't given that option, not by any stretch of the imagination.

There is a lot to say on the question of the whole MMR issue. It is an emotive subject and there does appear to be a conspiracy of silence. Tony Blair and Gordon Brown both still refuse to say whether their sons have received the triple jab and if, as their Government advocates, there is no problem with the vaccine, why do they both have a problem admitting that their sons have had it? Because they haven't is the obvious answer.

Dr Andrew Wakefield is a lovely, charismatic and caring doctor who has been discredited by the medical profession in this country for daring to try and prove that the MMR vaccine does cause autism and bowel disease in some children. He has had to leave the UK and take his family to America. He has had death threats made against him and for what? For trying to help a group of vulnerable people who are ill? Isn't that what he trained as a doctor to do? It makes you question where the real power lies. Is it by any chance with the drug companies who stand to lose a lot of money if liability is proved and compensation is payable? Is there a cover-up? We don't have a personal axe to grind, thank God, but this country is a democracy and yet this issue has been dealt with in a very undemocratic and personal way.

My own view is that any child with an auto-immune problem is vulnerable to more serious side-effects, particularly when their immature little immune system is already under threat from within. It shouldn't adversely affect the overall vaccination programme if those children who are potentially vulnerable were identified at GP level and given single jabs. It would restore confidence, help the take-up rate and eliminate the threat of an epidemic of measles, mumps or rubella, wouldn't it? (If that is a very simplistic view then I apologize to the medical profession, it makes sense to me.)

Luke had developed really awful weeping, sore eczema as a result of the epilepsy medication and he has just grown out of it. It has at times been infected, bleeding and has driven him and us absolutely mad. A lot of the medication we were prescribed actually seemed to make it worse, particularly the bath oils, which appeared to exacerbate the itching. Luke still avoids soap (don't most boys) and I stick to the same washing liquid and products. Even Luke's skin hates change. Swimming pools abroad make Luke itch like crazy, they must use different chemicals or concentrates, and much as he loves swimming, he usually ends up having to avoid the pool, which always seems so unfair.

Actually, eczema has been a major problem over the years because it would suddenly flair up out of nowhere, usually when we were somewhere different, making Luke very miserable and itchy. If Luke is miserable then we all are. He makes sure of that. We used to tell him to throw his itches away and he tried to, vigorously. Trying to identify the cause of the latest flair-up was difficult and Luke sometimes used to scratch all night, often until his skin was raw and bleeding. We had to take a full complement of creams, emollients, steroid lotion and calendula cream with us wherever we went.

I had forgotten just how bad it was until I met a lady the other day whose daughter had been at school with Luke when they were five years old. She said to her daughter, "you remember Luke - with the eczema," and that memory trigger also reminded me that he is mostly free of it now. Thank God. It really was a horrible curse for him and he used to look so pathetic with it all over his face and especially around his eyes.

Whilst in hospital, Luke would suddenly let off a high-pitched scream. It wasn't a distressed scream, more an excited scream. He still does sometimes let off the same scream, much like a gibbon really. Nowadays he will apologise afterwards. It takes him as much by surprise as it does us and he knows that I hate it, it makes me jump and has an eerie quality to it that makes my skin prickle. He also used to bend away from me when I held him and we nicknamed him the 'banana baby'. He was never cuddly, always squirming and wriggling to get away.

I can cuddle Luke now. It has taken eleven years to cuddle my boy. Sometimes this has been the worst part of all. Especially when he has been hurt or upset. He has never been able to be held or cuddled or even comforted but two years ago, something lovely happened. First of all he would back into me and I could hold him from behind for a second or two. Then he started to put his arms round me and squeeze me, very hard, so I could hardly breathe. Now he tells me "I need a hug" and those words are so fab, so worth waiting for. I am allowed to put my arms around him and he snuggles in for what feels like a fraction of a second before pulling away. Lately the hugs have been reciprocal and that is something that is beyond all expectations and is very precious. The only downside is that he does sometimes wake up at 2am and demand a hug, literally! Who knows what tomorrow may bring? Knowing Luke, I bet his girlfriends get all the cuddles and I get his dirty washing. Why change the habits of a lifetime?

Back to those baby days. We waited anxiously for all the milestone tests, terrified that these would indicate that Luke had sustained some brain damage during his illness and long periods of unconsciousness. It took 45minutes to revive him once. He passed all the progress tests with flying colours. He sat up at six months but was too impatient to crawl. He bypassed normal crawling altogether, preferring instead to pull himself up on the furniture and drag himself around on two legs. We thought this was brilliant, he was so advanced that he didn't want to crawl! And bearing in mind that we were watching closely for signs of brain damage, the fact that he appeared more advanced than he should be was very encouraging. We now know that crawling is a vital and important part of the brain's development. It is a highly complex cross-coordination motor movement that can't be replaced in a child's early development. Yet the intelligent part of Luke's brain realised that he couldn't achieve that degree of complexity of movement and found an alternative! Or is he just programmed differently?

He had already learnt to navigate the stairs and when he ran across the room at just ten months old we were delighted, initially. He seemed determined to explore not just the other side of the room but the other rooms in the house, and beyond. I soon realized that this was very hard work, keeping track of him. He never stayed still and would climb out of his cot and anything else that was meant to keep him contained. He had absolutely no sense of danger and to a great extent he still doesn't, although that is developing now, better late than never.

One morning I was desperate to wash my hair, so I put Luke into the travel cot in the spare bedroom and shut the door. I had an anxious and hurried shower and, still wrapped in a towel, ran to the spare bedroom. There was no sound and as I was expecting him to be protesting loudly at being left alone, my heart started to thump with the prospect of finding him unconscious. I learnt something that day that is still true today. If you can't hear Luke and he's not unconscious then he's doing something he shouldn't be doing. I can still remember the shock when I opened the door. Luke was sitting in the middle of the guest bed, having somehow hauled himself out of the travel cot, totally disinterested in the baby toys left there for him. He had spotted a big tub of *Sudacrem*, which I had left on the bedside table. *Sudacrem*, for the uninitiated, is a wonderful thick white cream that mums use on small babies for everything. (It works on spots too!)

It has the ability to create a layer of impenetrable thick white cream on everything it touches and this pot had touched everything. It was all over the quilt cover and all over Luke. His hair, which always stood on end, stayed flat to his head for weeks! The quilt cover ended up in the bin after several washes and that was the start of Luke's disasters. I took a photo at the time because I couldn't imagine anyone believing that a ten-month baby could cause such havoc in such a short space of time. Little did I know then how much Luke would cost us in damages alone. We have learnt that damage limitation is the best we can hope for.

Jan's tip: Homeopathy works really well for a child like Luke. It helped with his eczema and he seems particularly sensitive to it, especially the *suggestion* of it helping him.

Diprobase is the best emollient we have come across for his skin and we have tried everything.

Never underestimate the power of motivation. Luke can seemingly achieve the impossible if *he* wants to and a sense of humour has been essential to me in coping with the aftermath of Luke's chaos. It is also the key to him and it's a shame that the education system can't tap into that part of his brain to get him to school each day.

Luke's tip: when I was little my mum used to put me in the bath but she always had the water too hot and it made my itches worse. My itches used to drive me mad. It used to feel like my blood was itchy and not just my skin and when my face was hot and puffy I remember that I tried to scratch it off and get a new one that didn't itch. Strangely, I miss my itches now because they were familiar and scratching used to give me something to do with my hands. I have had a flair up lately in the creases of my arms and I won't put any cream on because I like the familiar feeling of scratching. Familiar things make me feel safe. If I see someone with eczema though I feel sorry for him or her. That is because I had it and so I do understand what they feel like. That is the only way I can feel for someone else. I have to know what it feels like; I can't imagine other people's feelings no matter how hard I try.

CHAPTER 4 SAVOUR THE MOMENT

As Luke became a toddler his frantic behaviour and frenetic levels of activity, combined with him not sleeping, were utterly exhausting. Added to that was the fact that I was now pregnant with Abbi and we were in the process of having a house built, having decided to leave the city for life in the country. I had been feeding Luke in the night and actually watched several ram raids and even a mugging from the bedroom at the front of our house in the heart of the suburbs in Bristol, a supposedly 'nice' area to live in. The overwhelming emotion though, no matter how exhausted I felt, was still one of relief that Luke was now, to all intents, well and healthy.

I should say here that when Luke was admitted to hospital I prayed like I had never prayed before. Although I had always believed in God, having had a strong Christian brethren background, my understanding of God then was that He had such high standards that I could never live up to them. I was a born rebel and I mistakenly thought that you only went to church if you were good, which I blatantly wasn't. (The fact that as children we were made to walk there, probably about two miles each way, three times every Sunday was enough to put you off too.) Now I know that church is a place for everyone, anyone, the imperfect, even the rebels like me. In the same way as hospitals are for the sick, churches are for the sinner. You go there to be healed by the expert, God Himself. So, when there isn't another human being on earth that can help you, when not even the doctors caring for your child can offer any treatment or prognosis apart from a 'wait and see' approach and you are talking about your child's life or death situation, who else do you turn to? I promised God that if He spared Luke's life I would always include Him in my life and I have kept my word.

Actually, my faith has proved vital to me, not only in coping with Luke, but also in the friends and people who God has brought our way to support us. I talk to God constantly and my understanding of Him now is one of a Heavenly Father who only asks that I believe in His son Jesus and accept His forgiveness. Being a Christian isn't about perfection, it's about forgiveness and Luke has taught me more about forgiveness than anyone can begin to imagine. (My neighbours and children will tell you that I am as far from perfect as it is possible to be! I can match Luke swear word for swear word and that is to my shame, but he would try the patience of a saint, which I most certainly am not. Not for the want of trying though.)

So on 26 March 2004 Abbi was born. Her birth was a doddle compared to Luke's. I was strolling around the hospital grounds with my sister Libbi when I felt a strong urge to push her out and some builders who were working on the front of the building at the time held the door open for me with a look of horror on their faces. A sense of male panic hung in the air as I waddled back into the hospital, clutching my swollen belly, ready and willing to push this new addition out. She was a big baby; 8lbs 9ozs of feminine tranquility, and her birth was utter bliss after the trauma of delivering Luke. I was well enough to enjoy her instantly and that has been a constant ever since. Luke and Paul were in another room at the hospital watching the Grand Prix practice session. I remember that Luke's eczema was awful and he kept trying to scratch his little face off. Abbi slept from the moment she was born at 4.30pm. I was kept in hospital overnight and the nurse kept telling me to wake her up and feed her. Having spent so many hours trying to get Luke asleep, only for him to wake up the moment I tiptoed out of his room, I just smiled sweetly. Yeah right! Sweet dreams.

My elder sister Fran, who is a GP, and her husband David did the second best thing that anyone could have done for me at that point. They offered to take Luke away with them for a few days so that I could spend some time getting to know Abbi and just get some rest. I think that is the one and only time that anyone else has had Luke for longer than two nights willingly! His reputation precedes him still. Paul, it should be said, has always been a workaholic and running his own business was a full-time commitment, which left little or no time for family life then. His entire family is the same and we even got married on a Sunday so that no one had to miss out on a day's business! My sister Libbi, (my birthing partner) did the best thing, staying with me, cooking, cleaning and protecting me. She is two and a half years younger but has always been taller than me and we have been best friends since childhood, no matter what.

When Luke came back from his five-day holiday, Fran had written a diary of his activities so that I could imagine what he had been up to. Just reading it exhausted me! I still find Luke totally exhausting when I haven't been with him for a while and he bursts back into my life, full of energy and non-stop LOUD talking. Only last night we had the same old conversation about his loudness, his lack of volume control and he gets really mad because, to him, his voice is normal, whatever that means to Luke. He doesn't hear his own voice. I have said time and time again "Luke you are shouting" and he says " No I'm not, this is shouting" and he then proceeds to shout very loudly with a lot of anger. It has taken me the longest time to realise that, because he is so literal, what I needed to say was "Luke, your voice is coming out loudly". That is the truth and he is dead right, he isn't shouting. Shouting to him is an emotional thing, an angry thing. Now we try and have whispering days so that he gets used to talking at a lower volume, but I can't report a great deal of success so far! I'm sure that a speech therapist would have some training techniques but we have never been lucky enough to have access to one.

Luke hated Abbi! He didn't really speak until she was born when he was two years and three months old, but he had a vocabulary in his head all stored up to come out when it needed to and flip me, it needed to now. He told me that he wanted to send her back to the hospital. He wanted her back in my tummy, anywhere but here. He also said that he would kill her, take a big knife and cut her up. *He meant it.* For the first year of her life I couldn't leave her alone with Luke. If I went to the toilet, she came. If I had a shower, she came. Otherwise, Luke came. I didn't trust him alone with her for a second.

It was about this time that Luke started to do a runner. The slightest thing would trigger him off and he would just run. It was like a reflex action and he was so fast. Several times I had to abandon Abbi in her pram and just run like crazy to catch him. He stopped running away about a year ago. Until then, he would just leg it. Run as far as he could until he was far enough away. Sometimes that would be in the next street, sometimes round the next corner but when he was little it would be until he was out of sight. The occupational therapist we saw years later told me that Luke's fight or flight response is primed and ready to go at all times. That in itself has to be exhausting. It is the body's adrenaline-fuelled reaction to an extreme situation, yet to Luke, all of life is lived at that extreme. That's why he either lashed out or legged it! It has been, for him, a primeval reflex response to a given situation that he can't control. Understanding why he did it didn't help me run any faster though!

Luke still remembers the intensity of his jealousy towards Abbi. She took my attention and he thought that it belonged solely to him. He hated the change in the dynamics of our relationship and he hated sharing my love with her. One day I had left Abbi sleeping in her pram and Luke was with me. He must have moved so fast that I didn't realise he had gone until I heard Abbi scream. Luke had taken a piece of chain that he had found and hit her clean across the head with it. The mark it left was a smidge away from her eye and had drawn blood right across her little forehead. It left me in no doubt that he did intend to hurt, even to kill her if he could. I am always on alert. Never relax when Luke is in the house, even now. He still does feel that he should have all the attention and he still tries to get it, any which way he can. He will tell you that he *needs* it. I think he does.

SAVOUR THE MOMENT

Keep the curtains pulled and don't let in the light

Hold off the day a little longer

Breathe slowly and count to 10 or 100

None of it makes any difference

Savour the moment

A whirlwind, a snatching of breath

A tornado even, a vortex of energy

Enters the room - the curtains go back

The light streams in and the force of it lands

Full pelt in my eyes

Recoiling from the sheer bravado, the boldness

I laugh, a little hysterically perhaps

Or just with the nervous knowledge of days gone by

It's my son, my boy woken from sleep

Demanding, so energetic, so forceful

Is it a good day? Is it a bad day?

Not that it makes any difference

Bad days become good days and good days become bad days

Just like that

No warning

No planning

No control

Just go with the flow, be pulled in its' wake.

Luke used to wake up at 5am; no matter how little sleep he had had during the night, he didn't actually sleep through the night until he was five years old, not once. Abbi, on the other hand, slept through the night from five weeks old!

Jan's tip: I didn't ask for help in those early days. I didn't let on how very hard it was and I don't think I really knew how to show my vulnerability. The people who love you are there for you *but* when you appear to be coping it is hard to break in with an offer of help. I was permanently exhausted and I thought everyone saw that. I call it the Joan Collins syndrome - Put your face on and keep smiling, because that is my way of coping. It's only looking back that I wonder just how I kept going. The lack of sleep was so exhausting in itself without having to keep up with Luke's very demanding behaviour all day, plus looking after Abbi and mostly without help from Paul who was absent for long periods of time through work. (Having said that, you can't wear your heart on your sleeve either and at 5am in the morning, there really isn't anyone to help you.)

I used to try so hard to keep up appearances. A tidy house is a lovely thing and it is hard to accept the mess but with Luke that is the only option. He is, and always has been, the world's messiest boy. He is pathologically untidy and a clean space is an open invitation to him to create havoc. That is as true now as it was when he was a toddler and just as frustrating. To try and keep on top of his mess is the best I can hope for but he can wreck a room in five seconds flat and a whole house in little more. So my advice is to relax your standards and be realistic about what you can cope with. If you are ok with it, so will everyone else be. Don't suffer in silence. I have found that most people are very kind if you explain the problem to them and they are pleased to be told. Be kind to yourself and know when you are close to the point of no return. Our GP is a good 'last resort' listening ear and although he doesn't have any resources to offer me, at least he understands and recognises the sheer physical cost of being Luke's mum.

Luke's tip: Even when I am tired my brain won't give my body a holiday. I can only switch off by watching TV. I get on my own nerves with my constant activity and I wish that I could relax. I can't sit on the sofa until I have taken all the cushions off and thrown them on the floor and made the room the way I want it. I have to have the door shut when I am in a room and all the lights on too. My brain can't accept another reality and that drives my mum crazy. It drives me crazy but that is how I first learnt to watch TV and I have to do things in the same way otherwise it feels all wrong and I can't settle and then I get very angry. When I get very angry I smash things and then the world falls apart and I am sorry afterwards but that doesn't mend the smashed things. I have smashed my mobile phone about five times and my glasses the same and then I can't see and I can't receive messages or phone my mum when I need her. How dumb is that? That is true of my whole life. The first way that I did something is the way I have to do it but I am using the logical part of my brain now to try and change things. If I am really stressed though I have to go back to the beginning. The worst part about being me is that I don't like me. I get on my own nerves but I can't control my behaviour and that is awful. It makes me want to hurt myself and sometimes I bang my head hard or I think about killing myself. I have written my will just in case I succeed one day.

Abbi's tip: My mum always takes my side if Luke has hit me. She always says that IT IS AN ABSOLUTE RULE THAT YOU DO NOT HIT GIRLS. Because Luke breaks all the rules he has hit me more times than I want to remember but he knows the rule and when he has hit me, mum ignores him and comes to comfort me. Then she talks to Luke about it and sometimes she really shouts at him because she is very protective of me. Luke says sorry afterwards, once his anger has gone because that is what he has been taught to do, but sometimes it is too soon for me. He gets really angry then, if he is saying sorry and I can't accept his apology. He thinks it is a fact that when you do something wrong, you say sorry and that makes it is better. He doesn't have any emotions about it and so he doesn't get it when mine are still upset. I have learnt that it is best to accept his apology because otherwise he gets mad about that too and off we go again! I am not so frightened of him now though because as I get older he is learning to respect me and he doesn't actually want to spoil the relationship we are getting. He knows that I understand him and I can hate his behaviour, but I do feel sorry for him too, because I know, like Mum, just how hard he finds life and how upset he is with himself afterwards when he has lost control. Sometimes I look into his eyes and see fear or loneliness but as soon as you show him kindness he sees that as weakness and asks you for something or tries to get you to do something for him.

CHAPTER 5 CONSEQUENCE, CAUSE AND EFFECT

Abbi was three months old and our new house was ready. Paul had bought a plot of land at auction, in a village called Hullavington in Wiltshire, whilst I was on holiday in Fuerteventura for a week with Luke and two of my three sisters. That in itself was an experience as, although he was only a toddler, Luke didn't like being somewhere different and just wouldn't sleep so I was absolutely shattered whilst my sisters were tanned, gorgeous and relaxed. I hated them! Abbi wasn't even a thought process at the time we started building. It was fun, finding Gordon, our builder and designing our very own house but it took a lot longer than we thought and there was always a problem or three to overcome, either with the planners or with the building, or the sub-contractors. Finally though, it was time to move in. We were given 24 hours by the council to give our house a name or they would allocate it a number. What do you call a house when you haven't lived there, it's brand new with no real characteristics and it isn't a cottage? We weren't inspired and every name seemed fanciful or unsuitable. Eventually we came up with **'The Edge'**. The house was right on the edge of the village; the planners had said that to us several times. "No, you can't add this feature, or that feature because the house is on *the edge* of the village and it needs to blend in with the countryside, blah, blah, blah".

Planners are very full of their own self-importance and if you let them think that you actually believe they are that vital to the grand scheme of each and every little detail, they become quite human and relax the rules a little!

We have lived life, as Luke does, literally, on the edge at **'The Edge'** and I have wished ever since that we called it something/anything else. Shalom - meaning Peace, that would have been better, much better.

There are several little holes in the upstairs walls at **'The Edge'**. In the week we moved in, Paul had been drilling around the rooms putting fixtures in place, so the sound of the drill was nothing unusual. I was feeding Abbi downstairs when Paul walked into the room and yet the drill was still going strong somewhere upstairs. Luke, aged two and a half, was up there all alone, holding the electric drill and happily drilling his way into the wall at his height level. He was both strong and steady, better with a drill at that age than I am even now. He was so determined to make his mark, even then and he obviously felt very important, imitating his dad.

The next day my mum came to visit. She walked downstairs looking a little flustered and beckoned me to go with her. Luke was at the top of the stairs with a tube of toothpaste that he was happily rubbing into the brand new carpet that Paul had just fitted, with my toothbrush. All it took was to take your eyes off him for a second and he was causing havoc. He was only two and a half then but he's still a master at it and he's had lots of practice. Another day he used a wax crayon to scribble big swirls of wax all over the new carpet in the lounge. My lovely friend Kyla advised me to iron his handiwork onto greaseproof paper. It worked and used up a whole roll in the process.

He graffitied the entire play-room one day with felt tip pens and we left it that way as a tribute to Luke's destructive abilities. When we did decide to repaint the room it had to be glossed as the only way to cover over the scribble that extended to the ceiling. He also decorated the white roof liner in our Shogun one day, having picked up a marker pen on his travels and used it to good effect. His handiwork knocked eight hundred pounds off the price when we came to trade it in.

Luke loved to watch videos (in the days before DVDs) and he would have to watch the same video again and again and again. His favourites were, predictably, *Thomas the Tank engine, Postman Pat* and *Top Gear*. He could repeat the entire script verbatim of each video, the whole thing, long before he possessed the equivalent vocabulary. The *Top Gear* script had several words that he couldn't possibly understand but he remembered them and repeated them just the same, including all the technical data which sounded very impressive. He told me the other day that there are 350 episodes of *The Simpsons* and he has every episode that he has watched catalogued in his memory. He is a brilliant mimic and will follow me around the house, repeating whichever episode has come to mind. He will start with "did I tell you?" and we all know what's coming next "about the episode of *The Simpsons* where…" and he then proceeds to relate the episode, in character and once he has started he can't stop! How much capacity does his brain have for storing information?

Until very recently, his evening schedule revolved around watching *The Simpsons*. Sacrosanct. Non-negotiable. He has learnt more about life from *Matt Groening* than I could ever teach him and he appreciates the humour immensely. He can do a mean *Marg Simpson* and would be brilliant at voice-overs if the present ones out price themselves.

He broke the video machine about four times before we discovered video locks. At £80 a time to repair it, and the aggro of no video machine to keep him quiet for an hour at a time, it was an expensive and very frustrating thing to do. We didn't realise what he was doing at first but then he explained. He was posting letters to *Postman Pat* into the slot. He thought that *Pat* was literally inside the machine!

Luke has the attention span of a flea. However, when he is watching something, even if he has seen it 100 times before, he is totally absorbed and does not hear or see anything else. He gets SO mad when you interrupt his viewing, it insults him, upsets him and disturbs him. There is no reasoning over this issue, it is a fact. He does not have the capability to switch his attention from where his brain is fixated. I have switched the TV off to get his attention, only to initiate world war three. His brain is so inflexible on this issue and others! It doesn't make any difference if you try and warn him that is what is going to happen because you have to switch off to deliver the warning. If you really need to, then you just have to do it and bear the consequences, not pretty.

Luke is highly intelligent. However his brain does not make the connection between what he does and what happens next as a consequence. This seems perverse but it is true and the longer I have lived with him, the more I realize that he really does not possess this natural ability to make connections. So he doesn't appear to learn by his mistakes and has no organisational skills whatsoever. As just one tiny example, we have a basket inside the front door for his shoes. Right inside the front door. Every day when he comes home, (that's IF he has been to school) be it as a tornado of energy or an angry boy who stomps off upstairs to be alone, he kicks his shoes off anywhere. Whichever version of Luke comes home, I don't think he has ever put his shoes in the basket and yet every day I say "Luke put your shoes in the basket". He never does. Consequently, every morning, unless I have tripped over them and put them in myself, his shoes are missing from the basket. You would think that eventually Luke, being smart, would get the message:- putting shoes in basket at night means finding shoes in basket next morning. Simple. This applies to everything. Most parents of boys, especially teenage boys relate to this but it really does apply to everything in Luke's case, including himself. He forgets to brush his teeth, brush his hair, get dressed, everything. All Luke's possessions fall where they are discarded and all the patience and training in the world fail to get the desired result. It would be so much easier to do everything for

Luke but then how will he ever learn? He gets so mad when his shoes are not in the basket every morning. "Where are my ****ing shoes?" he will shout angrily, for all the world as though he has put them in the basket and they have escaped to spite him. It happened again this morning. We end up hunting for his shoes to save him getting really agitated. If he gets too agitated the whole day is ruined for all of us. Multiply that by all the other things that Luke needs to take with him, his wallet, watch, glasses, bag. No matter that you have tried to organise him, he has moved everything anyway. As I say, damage limitation is the best we can hope for.

A lot of Luke's 'accidents' have been caused by this lack of connection of cause and effect. His friend James 'bigfoot' (Luke renames everyone close to him) came to tea one Monday evening when they were about seven or eight years old. Luke had a pedal go-kart that was his pride and joy and he and James were playing outside on the drive. The drive at **'The Edge'** is quite long and has three lamppost lights along its' length. I never relax when Luke has a friend around and especially James, as Luke can, and usually does, get over-excited and things happen.

Well, on this particular day I didn't sense any additional tension going down and must not have checked on the proceedings for a while. When I did look outside I spotted that one of the drive lights was missing. Upon investigation, I found a rope tied to the back of the go-kart and the missing light, wires and all, being dragged across the grass, with James steering and Luke pushing. James looked very worried, realising that all was not well but Luke was really happy because he had calculated that if they applied the right amount of force, this was exactly what would happen. The light would have to leave the ground. When I asked Luke what his father would say about the gaping hole and missing light, Luke began to see that perhaps it wasn't such a triumph. Until that point he had absolutely no idea of any other consequence than the satisfaction of testing out his theory. He loves to be right! Funnily enough the postman drove over one of the lights and did an equally good demolition job on it. Luke was delighted because that meant he was vindicated in his eyes. Because he does things deliberately, he thinks everyone else does too and he doesn't accept that accidents happen, although because of his lack of co-ordination he is the most accident-prone boy I know!

Luke has scribbled on every wall, he has made holes in every wall, every piece of clothing, he has dug huge holes in the garden looking for treasure, he has smashed doors and furniture and created untold havoc and he never stops in his quest for a new thrill. One day when he was three and a bit and Abbi could just about speak she said to me "Yuke stuck". He was indeed. He had climbed up the elderflower tree in the back garden and slipped. Fortunately, his trousers had been speared by a branch halfway down and he was dangling in mid air, saved by his trousers. Abbi has been his carer in a way ever since.

His father still finds it hard to believe that Luke doesn't understand consequence when he (Paul) has had to deal with the expensive consequences of Luke's behaviour. He also didn't get just how much damage Luke can do in a very short space of time. Turn your back for a moment and pay the price. I used to feel guilty that I had taken my eyes off him, if only for a minute or two and usually when I was on the phone. That reminds me, Luke can't bear me being on the phone. He has always tried to get my attention and still does, if I am on the phone. If he failed to cut me off, sometimes literally, sometimes by being noisy or hitting me or generally making a nuisance of himself then he would go off and noisily cause havoc elsewhere instead, knowing that I would be wondering what he was up to and would have to cut short my call. Now when I think back, I am amazed that I have managed to do anything else. It's much harder work than a full-time job but the hours are lousy, the pay is non-existent and the rewards are more of the same.

We went through a spate of getting punctures in our car tyres. Not every week, but every other week probably. Not all of them flat tyres, but slow punctures. After the sixth puncture Paul realised that all the punctures were being caused by nails and what's more that the nails were all the same and what's more again, that they were his nails from his garage. Luke, of course. Anything happens, just blame Luke. It usually is. Trouble is, his reputation precedes him and inevitably he gets the blame, sometimes unfairly. His sense of outrage is total when that happens. It is hard to live down a reputation though and as the saying goes 'mud sticks'.

Most of the time, Luke is trying to make sense of things that to him, don't make sense. He only sees life from his perspective, which to all intents and purposes can appear as selfish or manipulative behaviour. So as a consequence (which he doesn't do!) he tries to impose his control. He looks at the world differently, seeing unconnected ideas and unrecognised events which, with his particular logic, he tries very hard to make sense of by testing out "what happens if" to get at the bigger picture. Unfortunately, that often means damage and always mess. If he is looking for something, even now, the whole contents of the cupboard or drawer come flying out in the search for whatever it is that he wants. It's called straight-line thinking. I think!

Just the other Sunday I went to church with Abbi, leaving Luke home alone. That is our only option now, because if Luke doesn't want to leave the house, nothing short of a miracle can make him change his mind. I needed to go to church to pray for a few miracles for good measure and also to ask for forgiveness for my distinct lack of patience that week. Abbi had been very sick and Luke still demands as much attention as ever so I had been tired and grouchy which affects everyone. We came home to find that Luke had decided to make his dad a birthday cake in our absence. It took me three hours to clean the kitchen up from his efforts and that is the truth. There was even chocolate cake mix in my computer printer.

My friend Bernadette popped in just after Abbi and I had arrived home from church. Whilst I was registering, with shock, but no surprise, the mess that took out my plans for a *relatively* restful Sunday afternoon, Abbi complimented Luke on his cake. She is so good at understanding him. It was a triumph for Luke, particularly in terms of thoughtfulness towards his dad, holding his attention span long enough to finish it and the sheer effort he had expended. Selfishly though, it was no triumph for me and my heart sank as I struggled to remember that I had just asked for forgiveness for last week's lack of patience. Bernadette said that she would never again moan about the mess her two boys make! I had to completely reorganise the kitchen as all the cupboard contents had been pulled out in Luke's search for the right ingredients, which included vegetable oil, so as you can imagine, the floor resembled a chocolate skating rink.

He is learning to connect facts though and I am sure that if he had the right training a long time ago by someone other than me, he would be a lot better at it. My voice is so familiar to Luke and it is too soft. He has told me that. He responds much better to male voices because they sound 'serious'. I used to say to Luke, for example, "will you stop doing that, please Luke". He would ignore me until eventually I would get cross and shout "Stop that now Luke". Then he would respond. He has since explained to me that by saying "will you, please" in a normal i.e. soft voice it didn't sound like a command, just an option to which he chose not to respond, in fact not even to hear. A direct command in a serious voice however, demands a response. So politeness is wasted, totally, on him! It still is. Minimum of words gets maximum results and better to sound at the very least cross, but deep down mad and angry works best! Mrs. Thatcher learnt that when she was Prime Minister - if you want to be taken seriously in a man's world, lower the octave, fix them in the eye and look and sound fierce.

Jan's tip: Abbi and I have started to go out now that Luke is older and leave him home alone as that is the only way we can have a life. Sometimes Luke only feels safe at home and he can't bear any social contact so he refuses to get dressed on his anxious days. No one else sees him like that. What he is wearing is Luke's way of making a statement and he is very literal about it. Pyjamas mean 'not going anywhere'. However, by leaving Luke at home I have to be aware of the possible consequences. There is usually a price to pay because being 'home alone' is an invitation to him to explore other possibilities that are usually out of bounds and, because he doesn't do consequence, he won't think about my reaction, just about his pleasure. So although I appear to be enjoying myself at whatever it is we are doing, a part of my brain and Abbi's too, is constantly worrying about what we are coming home to. Acceptance is the key here. We have to accept whatever we find because that is the price for having a life. Sometimes the price feels too high but it is our only option and safety is the real worry. The *absolute* rule in my absence is **no fire**.

Luke's tip: If I get an idea it fills up my brain. I get obsessed with it and there is nothing that can stop me once I want to do something. I just have to do it. I don't understand why everyone isn't like me because there is no way I can ignore what my brain is saying, it's impossible not to. My mum has sayings to repeat to me and she says "think before you blink Luke," to try and get me to stop and think what will happen if I do something. You can imagine that when I was smaller I used to think, then blink very hard and do it any way!

Now I just do it anyway because I am a teenager.

Some people make me very excited and James is one of them. I don't know why, but everything is louder, bigger, better when he is there. One day we did an experiment with vinegar and baking soda to show how excited I get compared to everyone else and my cup fizzed over everything. James' just bubbled a bit. That helped him understand me more because I can really get on everyone's nerves when I am excited and can't control myself. I haven't got an 'off' switch.

I love making people laugh and if someone laughs at me I used to do the same thing over and over to get the same response. Same if I told a joke and the person laughed, I would keep telling them that joke to make them laugh again. I find the same thing funny over and over again because that is how my brain is wired and I thought everyone was the same as me. My mum used to say to me, "once funny, twice not so funny, three times boring".

If someone tells me a joke then I laugh because I know that is why they have told it to me, to make me laugh, but then I sometimes spoil it by saying "I don't get it" after I laughed because I don't and then my friends get mad with me. They think I am lying when all I am being is diplomatic! Sometimes being sociable is just too much like hard work.

CHAPTER 6 LABELLING OF LUKE-ADHD

There was no question that Luke was hyperactive as a toddler, a baby even. He never stayed still, he hardly slept, as soon as he could physically manage it he was up and out of the door and by anyone's standards he was a challenge. At the Mother and Toddler group we attended he bashed and bit and hit to get the toy of his dreams, no matter who had it. More than once I had to apologize for his apparently aggressive behaviour, before he was even a year old. I tried to leave him at a private nursery, just to get a little rest time and to try and get a life again. That didn't work. He screamed the place down as soon as I walked out of sight and didn't stop until I got back again. They suggested that I try somewhere else.

Luke started at the Pre-school in our village when he was three years old. Fortunately for us, there were two lovely ladies who worked there. Ann had an autistic son and was so good with Luke. She called him her 'pickle sandwich' and she was the first person that Luke learned to love. He used to go to her house for tea and she was utterly patient with him, no matter what he touched or broke as he raced around her lovely tidy house. Sadly, she died of cancer over a year ago. Luke went to see her two days before she died. He knew she was dying, no one told him, he has an uncanny sixth sense. She realized Luke was different and although we didn't discuss his behaviour in any great detail back then, she understood him and accepted him, working with his behaviour, using humour and accepting his ways, which helped to relax him although he still put up a fight not to go every single day.

Gail also understood Luke and became a lifeline in the form of a babysitter. Because she was familiar, Luke would accept her for an evening and she also became a good friend. One evening she let Luke watch *Casualty* with her because he could never settle down to sleep, his brain was too hyper. She eventually put him to bed and came downstairs for a glass of wine and some relaxation. Luke got out of bed as soon as her back was turned and went into my bedroom with his life size monkey, who he chopped and cut and butchered to look like a casualty victim. To make it more realistic he took my red Estee Lauder lipstick and smeared great globs of it over the monkey, himself and the bed. He cut the monkey's ear off and hacked a great hole in its' chest, where he then stuffed an appropriately-shaped toy to look like a pacemaker. Amazingly, he can always find the right implements for destruction, if nothing else. He eventually fell asleep in the middle of his own casualty scene and that is what I found when I went to bed. Every picture tells a story! Everything Luke does has to be literal. No effort is spared in getting the right clothes or props to re enact a scene or create one from his imagination. He once cut up the king size sheet on our bed to make himself a long flowing cape. I've lost count of the number of times we have had the furniture rearranged to accommodate Luke's games. He has straight-line thinking. Has an idea, finds the props and makes it a reality.

Non-negotiable. His energy is amazing and no effort is spared creating the havoc that his brain demands. No energy is left over however, for clearing up afterwards!

Luke's behaviour at this time was impossible. The only predictable thing about him was/is his unpredictability and he was angry, itchy, destructive, demanding, and LOUD - what's changed? He started fighting me not to go to pre-school. This made life very difficult, with Abbi in tow, because he is so strong and I would have to drag him along and he would do a runner as soon as he could escape my hold. When we got there he would scream and beg not to be left. I always felt so guilty leaving him and would come home in tears, but for my sanity I had to have some respite from his chaotic and disruptive behaviour at home. (Little did I know then that at age thirteen, I would have to drag him out of bed each morning and he would still hate going to school and still be fighting me, most days.) I didn't know who to talk to or where to turn. Because he was my first child, although I instinctively knew there was a problem, the worry was always that it might be my reaction to him that was the problem, although I realise now that Luke's precarious start to life made it much harder for me to be objective about his behaviour. It was subjectively emotional, to say the least.

One morning I got Luke ready for pre-school under protest as usual. He was four years old. He has always had a big resistance to change and particularly to change that he doesn't choose. Every morning now is a struggle for him to adapt from the cozyness of his bed to a new day and he wakes up with a great deal of drama and swearing. The first thing that Abbi and I usually hear is loud swearing and abuse from Luke. (It is still horrible even when it is this familiar.) Only yesterday morning at 7am I went into his bedroom and stroked him to try and wake him gently and coax him into a new day. He swore very loudly and angrily and flinched at the touch of me, his mum. Once his conscious brain kicked in however, he apologised for swearing and rolled over to try and adjust to the facts of waking up. It is a big shock to his system.

This autumnal morning I had bought him a smart new coat from M&S with a lovely orange quilted lining. Shopping with Luke has always been a no-no, he is over stimulated at every aisle, so any clothes still have to be bought without him and he usually doesn't like them because he didn't choose them! I think that we had showed him his new coat but he wouldn't have tried it on. I was determined that he would wear it and he was equally determined that he wouldn't. We had a huge battle of wills and I eventually got him into the coat before he did his usual runner. As I was getting Abbi quickly bundled into her coat to chase him I realized that he had stopped running just outside the front door. He had pulled his new coat off and was stamping on it with all his might in the mud. He then proceeded to pee all over the lovely orange lining. I can still remember the absolute rage that I felt and all the frustrations of his awful behaviour became focused on that orange lining.

That was a defining moment for me in realizing that we needed help with Luke and that whatever was driving his behaviour needed a name. I now know that to Luke the coat felt like a strait jacket. It was stiff and unfamiliar and it restricted his movement. He panicked at the strangeness, the stiffness. Strong feelings call for strong language and if you don't have the vocabulary then how else do you communicate that you're peed off without peeing? Luke is so literal!

His clothes until now have always been easy to wear, non-restrictive and easy to throw off. They must still be non-itchy and if he doesn't like them then he won't wear them no matter what. Luke will never be a fashion victim but he does have a certain sense of style which suits him and he really likes 'formal'. He has always wanted to wear a shirt and tie because that is the uniform of a businessman, something Luke aspires to.

Our health worker came to see us at my request and immediately referred us to Dr Stuart Murray, Consultant Community Paediatrician for Bath who we now regard as a friend, we've seen him that often! (I've had more letters from him than anyone else in my life.)

He immediately diagnosed Luke with ADHD, his first label, and we had some therapy sessions for the whole family. Those were awful, we were closeted together in a small room and Luke behaved as badly as you would expect, given that we were all talking about his behaviour in front of him and there was no escape for a wildly hyperactive, driven and itchy little boy. The strange thing is that no matter who you are seeing in relation to your child's behaviour, you still want them to behave well, even though the professional needs to see their real behaviour in order to help. In our society, your child's behaviour reflects on your parenting, rightly or, in our case, very wrongly!

Luke almost punched Dr Murray in the face at one visit. Luke was asked by Dr Murray to demonstrate his reach by aiming at his face and stopping appropriately. The purpose of this was an ongoing test of Luke's spatial awareness and as he had none he didn't stop thrusting his arm until it was literally in Dr. Murray's face. To his credit, he only flinched slightly. As a parent I was mortified but also bemused that he hadn't seen it coming, I had but then I live with Luke and nothing he does surprises me any more.

He would always want a particular cup, plate, chair etc. and just wouldn't, *couldn't* accept any other reality than the blueprint in that inflexible brain of his. It was pointless trying to persuade him, distract him, tell him even - he was always beyond reasoning on such things. Luke has tested our patience to the sainthood stage. He pushes every boundary to understand where its' limits are. He asks every question. He uses every swear word. He never gives up, pushing and pushing for whatever it is that is imprinted on his brain at that time. If he wants to do something he sees absolutely no reason why he can't do it. As we say many times, "Luke, what part of No don't you understand?" to which he replies "the N".

Jan's tip: I think I have wasted so much time explaining things to Luke. He doesn't listen to me, tunes my voice out and what lots of words say to him are 'room for negotiation'. That gives his logic a reason to keep trying. I wish I had saved my breath and just said NO right at the beginning. But saved the Nos for when they really counted. You can't distract him so there's no point in trying and he can outlast any one when he is focused, obsessed with something.

> If you see a child behaving badly, before you make a safe and smug judgment on the parent's lack of abilities, consider that there may be another explanation and thank God it's not you and your child.

> It is very hard for families like us to get babysitters. We can't just have the 15 year old next door for an evening because of the responsibility of Luke and yet we need an evening off more than most parents. If we can find someone to 'Luke sit', we have to pay them well because it isn't your run of the mill stuff and you have to be prepared for any eventuality. It is probably the best thing that you could offer someone like me, an evening off with no worry attached and no emotional price to pay either.

Luke's tip: I hate the word NO. It is like a rag to a red bull. Seeing Dr Murray always stresses me out. No offence to him, but he has a small room with nothing to do and nothing to distract me, plus my mum has told him all the bad things about my behaviour. I behave sometimes as I think he expects me to, although I always apologize to my mum afterwards because I know that she would like me to be good. When I am stressed or excited I can't control my behaviour and that is one of the things that people don't seem to understand about me. I find contact with people very stressful, unless I am pretending to be someone else. O yes, I am considering a career as an actor because I bet lots of them are like me. When we see Dr. Murray it would be better if there were things for me to do and also if I didn't have to listen while my mum talked to him about me.

But I like him and he is a familiar part of my life. He makes my mum feel safe because he is the only person who understands when she tells him about my behaviour, he talks to lots of mums with children like me.

I am very destructive in lots of ways, I tear things, break things, chew things and cut things up and I don't usually realise what I have done until it is done. If I came to your house I would walk around touching things and my mum gets mad with me, very mad with me but I honestly do not know I am doing it. My mum says she only takes me back somewhere for a second visit to apologise for what I did the first time around. ADHD is so tiring and it is harder to live with than you think because I wear myself out but I can't stop myself.

CHAPTER 7 TURN ON THE LIGHT - LANGUAGE, LITERALLY

Language, and the use of it, when taken literally, doesn't always make much sense. We who understand the subtlety of language do so implicitly and so we don't appreciate what a huge gap it leaves when that sense is missing. This sense also includes spatial awareness, social timing, facial expression and body language. We take it for granted. It develops with our use of language. Luke possesses none of these skills.

For a start, Luke takes language very literally. So for example, when a teacher told Luke to pull himself together he was very confused as to what he was being asked to do. When I explained the meaning he was very insulted. (If Luke is insulted he bears a big grudge and he has to decide when to let that grudge go.) So there was not only an expression that he didn't understand how to interpret, just how do you 'pull yourself together?' but a big implied meaning which Luke found offensive. The implication being that he could do something about *who* he is, *how* he is. Because that is how he learnt about implied meanings, he thinks that all implied meaning is insulting and he thinks that when you say one thing you could well be implying another. Confused? So is he.

Sometimes his literal interpretation is amusing, sometimes touching. When our lovely friend and babysitter Gail lost her husband John, (he died very unexpectedly from a burst blood vessel) Luke was concerned for her. He does sometimes have feelings for other people and thinks quite deeply about death and loss and what that must feel like. He said to me "Gail will be all right because Scottish Widows will look after her". I realised that he had taken their TV advert quite literally for every widow. If only!

Indirect speech is another minefield. I woke up one morning with the words of a poem forming in my head and scribbled them down before Luke appeared and hijacked my thought process. The previous day Luke had been very cross with me. He had been learning about implied meaning at school and turned on me accusingly when I met him outside his classroom. He told me that I wasn't direct enough when talking to him, that he was always trying to work out what I really meant and it must have triggered something in the subconscious part of my brain.

'Turn on the Light'

You are you and I am me
I take your words literally
Your words to you make perfect sense
But words to me can cause offence
Hidden meanings lurk behind
The words of others in my mind
"It's dark in here" means that to me
"Turn on the light so I can see"'
Is what you really should have said
I can't read words inside your head
My brain doesn't work like yours
It doesn't close and open doors
Its door is OPEN WIDE or SHUT
It's BLACK and WHITE, it's in a rut
It doesn't jump from thing to thing
It doesn't have a central spring
I need the facts, I want to know
Exactly when and where and so
I scream and shout, I cry in pain
You have let me down again
To you it's words and words can change
Well my brain doesn't have that range
I need to know so I can cope
I can't survive on love and hope
Hope is not a word I feel
I only understand what's real
Real is fact and facts make sense
Of all those words that make me tense
Because I'm different you owe me
A very big apology!

This language stuff is so confusing for my boy. He continually asks questions. Are you being sarcastic? Why can't I say that? Do they mean…..? Are you insulting me? He asks that if I pay someone else a compliment when I am talking to him - "are you insulting me?" because he thinks that if I say someone else is lovely then I am implying that he isn't!

Luke lives on a knife-edge and we live there with him, all the time. Every social happening, big or small, is exhausting for him because he has to use extra resources to cope. Concentrating leaves him exhausted and yet his brain doesn't take up his body's messages so he doesn't know that he is exhausted and so he will keep going long after he should be asleep. That puts him in energy deficit for the next day and so on.

If someone asks him how he is, he tells them, long and loud! He assumes they are asking for the low down on his well-being. Why ask if you don't want to know? He finds it very confusing to understand social talk. See you later? No you won't. It makes conversation so fraught sometimes. He also gets very angry if you talk out of turn. When he is speaking he will lose his concentration if interrupted and so he can't tolerate interruptions. It is all so black and white. If you introduce a topic on which he considers himself an expert he will lecture you on the subject. It turns pleasant chitchat into the art form of being pedantic and you have to argue with him. Much as you don't want an argument, the only way to shut him up is to refuse to listen. "Shut-up Luke" we shout. It's language that can be taken literally. SHUTUP. The rest of the world aren't going there with him and he has to know that.

We have lots of memorable moments of Luke's literal understanding. On his fourth birthday he was promised that his dad would be home at six o'clock to share his birthday cake. Luke loved blowing out the candles, although with much spitting when he was younger because he finds it hard to blow. No one ever wanted a piece of his cake after he had finished the candle blowing, it looked like an invitation to eat spit and that suited him fine because he didn't want to share it anyway. It was *his* cake. Well this particular birthday he was waiting at the window from lunchtime on, looking for his dad. He asked me how he would know when six o'clock came so I drew him a picture of how the hands looked. The next thing Luke was shouting "it's six o'clock" and he took me to the clock. He had wound the hands on to six o'clock and with his literal understanding, he thought that if the clock said the right time then the right thing would happen!

Facial expression is something that Luke neither understands nor does. His face is usually very pale and expressionless. When he was a little boy we would tell him to smile for a photo. He always made this awful grimace and everyone, me included, thought that he was being awkward (as always) and making a silly face. (However, looking back I did have an instinct about it because I realized that to get a good picture of Luke we had to make him smile or laugh spontaneously.) "Take that silly look off your face and smile for the camera," we would say and he didn't know how to do either of those things so he would throw a wobbly. Voila, no happy family scene yet again, courtesy of Luke. Now when I look at photos of those days I feel so sad for him because he is making the same strange face in all of them. His brain didn't tell his face how to smile or maybe it is the other way round and his face doesn't get what his brain is telling him?

Luke's embarrassed face is a smirk. So he has been told off again by teachers for appearing to smirk when he has just been told off! He doesn't have a clue what his face is registering because his brain is working with the emotions of the situation. Particularly now he is older, this is tough because everyone assumes that he is choosing the face he is making, or making the face he is choosing. He's not. He doesn't have a clue what his face is doing because he is experiencing the strong emotions that disapproval engenders in anyone.

I understood about the grimace/smile when Luke was talking to me seriously. He usually asks to talk to me at bedtime and I have to go there because if he wants to talk it's a major achievement and I learn a lot about him, but it also delays his bedtime and he is well aware of that fact. However, if you ask Luke to talk to you at a convenient time you may as well forget it. It's always at the wrong time, usually when you're tired and don't want to but you have to. He's so contrary!

Talking Luke style is back to front. That is how I have learnt so much about him. His back to my front. He can't look at me and talk and this is deep stuff. Actually, the sight of his neck, all stiff and unyielding is very endearing and quite familiar. (Incidentally that is how he first learnt to accept a cuddle, he just backed into me after one of our talks and I held him for the briefest of seconds.) I learn such a lot from Luke about all sorts of things and he is very articulate and insightful into his own condition and also into other people's perception of him and his behaviour. In particular he knows the people who think well of him and he definitely knows those who don't and responds accordingly.

Anyhow this particular time, Luke agreed to show me his face after we had talked about expressions. We got a mirror and he could see what his grimace/smile actually looked like. Then he practised a proper smile. He could make exaggerated faces by thinking of a cartoon character who looked angry, happy, cross. We took the mirror away and I asked him to smile and the smile reached the corners of his mouth! Lovely moment. We did surprised, angry, cross - he produced all of these to order, although in a very exaggerated way but when I asked him to make a sad face he became agitated and turned his back to me. He explained, "I can't do a sad face because that means I'm depressed and now I feel happy. I don't want to feel depressed so why are you asking me to make a sad face?" Then I was reminded of just how complicated everything is when even your face has to be literal.

Mr Bean is someone who Luke understands very well and laughs at. He taught Luke about gesture, although it is far from subtle. In one episode he put the middle finger up, without realising what the gesture meant and Luke copied him literally, without having any idea of what it meant either. Lorry drivers became very aggressive to me when I was driving and it took me some time to realise why, Luke sitting in the back pretending to be *Mr Bean*, middle finger at the ready. Once I had explained to him what the gesture meant, he used it even more determinedly! Still does, loves the power it gives him.

If you don't look at someone when they talk, you miss out on all those subtle cues that their facial expression or body language give out. Luke finds eye contact difficult but not always for the reason you may think. Sometimes he just can't deal with the emotions that looking at a person bring out in him. But I have also realised that he can't see and listen at the same time. The face speaks one language and the voice another. If he is watching a face he is trying to read the 'face language' so he doesn't hear the words. If he is listening to words he is trying to work out implied meanings, indirect speech etc. so he can't watch the face otherwise he forgets to listen. It is too much information to process all at once (even if you are an expert at multi-tasking VHG style!) So if someone says to him "Look at me when I'm talking to you", which bossy grown-ups tend to do, he literally does that. He watches the face of the person doing the talking very, very carefully but he doesn't hear a word they say!

If, however, Luke is not watching you but is seemingly engrossed in his own world he hears the words perfectly. After numerous hearing tests it was decided that Luke is selectively deaf and he is. It is the motive for his selective deafness that we didn't get. He can either look or listen but he often can't do both so he selects the mode. He used to say that he could only hear with one ear.

Interestingly this does not apply to TV. Only to real people because real people require social interaction on his part which is the numero uno most difficult thing for him to do. That is why TV is so relaxing for him. It doesn't expect him to understand and respond correctly and so he can put the two things together with no emotional output and that is lovely for him. He learns so much from TV. It is also why cartoon characters and *The Simpsons* are so useful in his learning because they aren't subtle!

When Luke is following me around the house recreating for me an episode of *The Simpsons*, complete with accents and sound effects, he thinks that my enjoyment is matched only by his. I, on the other hand, take a leaf out of his book and go into deaf mode whilst watching his face to see his obvious enjoyment.

Luke doesn't understand that when you are in a different room to him, or outside when he is inside, that you can't hear him talking to you. He gets absolutely wild because he thinks you are ignoring him. No matter how many times we explain this, it just doesn't sink in. He also has no concept of you being asleep if he is awake. He will bound in to your room, switch on the light and start bombarding you with facts. When you say "Luke, you've just woken me up" he gets very indignant. "I did not, you were awake. Your eyes were open when I came in" he will say and he just doesn't get it. Drives you mad. Wake him up though and that is a very bad experience, every morning!

The saying 'In your face' was made for Luke. He is literally that. He doesn't have that nice little 'keep out' area of about eighteen inches which the rest of us like maintained around us at all times. No, he invades your space. He will actually try and walk straight through things to get to where he is going, people included. But he hates his space being invaded and hates being touched even by me, or sometimes especially by me, unless he is ready for it. He has no concept of queuing, waiting, taking turns, none of that means anything to him. It is a very hard thing to teach someone, he should have been born a German. They don't do queuing either! Actually, our very polite, reserved and aloof way of life is probably the worst culture for someone of Luke's temperament. He would be much more at home in the jungle, where boys can be boys and adventure and danger go hand in hand and you need your fight or flight response to be primed and ready for action and social niceties are only down to a matter of survival and spitting is probably a good thing to do. (Actually, he is more closely affiliated to the animal kingdom in my opinion.)

Jan's tip: The mirror is a good way of letting your child see what they look like and practising expression. I didn't realise for a long time that Luke had no self image at all and that he wouldn't recognise himself if he saw his own face out of context, say, in a magazine. It is helpful to draw faces and put exaggerated expressions to them as a crude way of identifying moods. Face language is very complex though and this is one of the areas in which I wish I had understood sooner that Luke needed help. I have been attending a parenting course recently and learning about the eyes. They are called the window to the soul because they do subtly give off clues all the time by where they are and what they are doing. If you can't look at someone when they are talking to you, you lose out on such a lot of that subtle information. Our children really do need education of a social kind in tandem with an academic education and they need speech and language therapy and specialist programmes to help them achieve their potential.

Luke has only just stopped vocalizing his entire thought process and he still does talk to himself a lot, probably as the safest person to talk to. His natural voice is very flat, almost a monotone with very little inflection and yet he is a brilliant mimic who can talk in any accent all day if he chooses to. When he felt the urge to swear, long and loud, he used to adopt a rich Scottish accent because he knows that Billy Connolly swears. He thought that it made it acceptable for him to follow suit if he sounded the same and it has been a good way for him to let off steam at home without being told off! If he swears *at* me however, I have every right to be upset and he understands that I take it personally and get mad with him.

To teach Luke to blow we got a feather and got him to try and blow it across the table and off the other side. That gave him an idea of how to blow more effectively, hopefully without spitting!

To teach him to blow his nose we used an Otovent that you can buy from the chemist. It is a balloon designed to help with glue ear. You place it over one nostril and block the other nostril off, before snorting down the nose and inflating the balloon. It is an exaggerated way of blowing with a visual result, which is Luke's way of learning. (The French prefer to use it instead of putting grommets in to treat glue ear in children.)

On the subject of TV, it would be easier for Luke to have a TV in his room and that will probably have to happen one day, but I have resisted so far because it has been a very important way of teaching him to share, to negotiate and to socialise. It is also a strong motivator in getting him to behave. If he is being really impossible I take the Sky card out and he has to earn it back, although the battle is hard won every time and I often collect some bruises in the process.

Luke's tip: I do find communication very difficult and my friends get cross with me when I say things that are sexist, racist or politically incorrect. I am not trying to upset people but I have strong opinions in my brain. I was born with them and I am trying, now I'm older, to use logic to change them. When I talk I have started to say things like, "I don't want to cause offence but I think....." or "In my opinion...." because then people realise that I am aware. Before I used to say my thoughts as facts and people would argue with me and get cross with me and tell me I didn't know what I was talking about. Although I have an excellent vocabulary, I find the art of conversation very difficult. I never know the right moment to speak and so I either butt in or lose my moment. This is very frustrating and then when I do say something I am speaking too loudly and what I say isn't the right thing. My friends insult each other and swear all the time but when I do those things I get told off for them. I don't really know when to say things and when not to and because I am impulsive I say whatever comes into my head and then people don't like me. For example if someone is fat

I say so. It is the truth but you're not allowed to tell the truth. My mum says don't lie and then people lie to each other all the time. Some days I don't want to talk to anyone because it is too much to cope with. The trouble is that I need to practise my social skills more, not less!

Abbi's Tip: Luke lectures me and I hate it. I tell him when he is being bossy and he is, very. He follows me round talking to me, telling me everything and he controls the TV and gets really mad if he can't watch his programmes that he wants to. We have to have our own viewing times but he still tries to take control over mine and when he is watching my programme he talks all the time but no one is allowed to make a sound when his programme is on. He only learns when someone does the same thing to him so that is what I do, bravely!

Last night I was in the bathroom getting ready for bed and Luke wanted to use the bathroom. He shouted and swore at me to get out of the bathroom immediately and started hammering on the door and he was very angry that I was in there. He acts like no one else has a right to do anything if it doesn't suit him. So I took twice as long as I would have done but that is against my nature. Mum says 'do as you would be done by', but that just doesn't work with Luke. You have to teach him by doing it back to him and that is mean really.

CHAPTER 8 BLACK AND WHITE

Luke has the long-term memory of an elephant and the short-term memory of a gnat. He can remember incidents from his first years of life in exquisite detail and yet he can't remember what he was asked to do in the last minute. He can't organise himself to save his life. He has no spatial awareness, drops, spills, breaks and loses everything and yet he can get into a go-kart and drive with skill and precision to win. He is actually a brilliant driver. My theory on that is that his brain works at such a fast pace that his body can't keep up, but give him speed and everything co-ordinates for him. He is very competitive and hates to lose, so there have been several tantrums of the worst kind, although he is learning now to compete with a degree of grace. Ayrton Senna was, reputedly, a lot like Luke as a boy and possessed that single-minded obsessive need to win. I guess he also didn't recognise danger.

Everything is one extreme or the other. There is no grey area.

He learnt to ski aged seven years and on his second day, we were asked to remove him from ski-school. He was so fast, fearless and disruptive that the instructor suggested his dad take him down the black run, which is all Luke was obsessed with doing as soon as he had mastered stopping. He did ski the black run and I have learnt not to watch because I am too terrified. Last time we went skiing, I ended up being skied down the mountain on a stretcher with a dislocated shoulder, (which is a *very* painful injury – it still hurts now) yet I am slow and steady compared to Luke!

In normal life he has broken both arms, burnt himself quite badly and had numerous scrapes and spills due to his lack of fear. The wonder is that he hasn't had more injuries actually.

He is wired up wrongly in all sorts of ways. His brain is the alternative version all right!

His pain threshold is completely odd. A small hurt would have him screaming in total panic as the shock registered with his nervous system and the sight of his own blood was enough to send him frenzied with fear.

Strangely though, he felt no fear in doing the craziest things which inevitably meant that he would hurt himself. Once hurt, he used to flap his hands and go into a total state of uncontrollable hysteria. He is learning to be macho now, peer pressure is a wonderful motivator for a teenage boy. A big hurt however, had the opposite effect and he would appear not to feel pain. When he broke his arm for the first time, aged five, I was in the shower and he had flung himself headfirst off the back of a chair in the living room. He called out to me "Mummy, I've broken my arm." "Yeah right Luke," I called back, not believing him because I thought that if he had, he would be hysterical as per normal.

I carried on having my shower and then came out to find him lying on my bed with an obviously very twisted and broken arm that made *me* want to get hysterical. He, on the other hand was very calm, very detached from the situation. He had to have his right arm straightened under general anaesthetic and put into plaster all the way up to the shoulder. One of the interesting things I noticed was that his eczema cleared up completely on that arm whilst it was in plaster, even though Luke had borrowed a knitting needle from his Gran to poke down the plaster and get at his itches. A broken arm didn't stop him doing anything, not a single thing; he just took over with the left one. We were going to Centerparcs the next day for my birthday so Paul taped Luke's broken arm up in a black bin liner and he whizzed up and down the rapids and slides in the swimming pool as usual, none the worse for fresh adventure. I think that a small hurt registers the shock with his nervous system much more than a big one, for some reason.

Luke cut his hand quite deeply on a tin recently so we popped off to our local casualty to get it properly looked at. The nurse on duty asked him lots of questions and he in turn asked her why she wanted to know everything that she has just asked him. Fortunately she was one of those people who sense the difference and go with the flow. Believe me, you love those professionals when you come across them because there are the other type who ooze disapproval and scare me rigid. Luke senses them a mile off and does his best to rattle them, usually successfully.

His impulsivity is calming down a bit with maturity. We have always said 'think before you blink'. Well he does a bit more now, unless he is so fired up that he is beyond reach, which happens but not as frequently. This is wonderful for Luke because his own behaviour has caused him acute embarrassment many times and the sheer frustration of not being able to control himself has led to yet more outbursts.

He still has big problems with attention and finds it impossible to sit still unless he is totally absorbed, usually when he is watching *The Simpsons*. If he is in a social setting then the pressure of trying to behave and sit still and be social are huge and he will find a way to focus his attention, either by scratching at his arms, chewing his clothes or scribbling on his hands if he can find a pen that he hasn't already chewed up.

Aged nine years was about the peak of his hyperactivity and although we had been offered *Ritalin* as an option before then, we were reluctant to take it until the day that Luke ran across the road and came within an inch of being knocked over. It gave the driver a terrible shock. He actually screamed because he thought he would hit Luke. Luke didn't know that he was going to run until he was running. That's how impulsive his brain was then.

We decided a drugged Luke was better than a dead Luke and so we started him on *Ritalin*, having been told to read up about it on the Internet before we made up our minds. Everyone's opinion is just that and obviously everyone reacts differently. There are times when you are desperate for some professional to say do this and you do it, without always having to take responsibility for the decision, especially when it is a big one.

It was a learning curve and the drug itself, even the slow release version, was in no way an easy option. For a start I had to go into school to give Luke his lunchtime dose because as a controlled drug no one was allowed to take responsibility for it. Also it gave Luke strange tics and his eyes kept blinking. He would say to me "my eyes are blinking" and they were, uncontrollably. The 'think before you blink' took on a whole new literal meaning. I made him wear sunglasses one day when they started rolling around in his head because it was so weird, it scared me. (I try to work on the basis of 'out of sight, out of mind' with Luke because otherwise you'd go insane with worry.)

He also lost his appetite completely. Bearing in mind just how limited his diet was anyway, due partly to his extremely over-sensitive sense of smell, this was a big problem. He said everything tasted wrong because it smelt wrong and one of the reputed side effects of *Ritalin* is that it stunts growth. From our experience it certainly acts as an appetite suppressant. At about 4pm each day Luke was completely hyperactive, on the rebound of the drug wearing off. This lasted all evening and meant that his sleep pattern went all out of sorts. A tired and hungry Luke was a nightmare of an angry sort. Most of the benefits were at school because he was so much calmer in the mornings, much less impulsive and more able to concentrate. His handwriting was so different whilst on *Ritalin* that it was hard to believe it was written by the same child. It was neat, small and really lovely. His books also were tidier, not chewed, scribbled on and messy. However, a more controlled Luke presented a different set of problems and it became apparent that ADHD wasn't the only thing affecting him. He started to become more anxious, aggressive and withdrawn without his naturally impulsive and frantic behaviour and I didn't know which was worse. A drugged Luke was a vulnerable Luke.

One of the positive side effects of *Ritalin* was that Luke's travel sickness cleared up completely whist he was on it. As soon as he stopped taking *Ritalin*, he started being travel sick again.

We did have a spell in the middle of all this where he was quite happy at home and at school and this was wonderful. He has always been difficult at home and reserves his best efforts for school, which is as you wish it. However, sometimes it was very frustrating, because at primary school everyone would tell me that he was fine, if very bright and energetic and I knew differently. Just couldn't explain his frantic or aggressive behaviour at home to anyone, out of respect for him really. You don't want to convince other people that your child is a monster, but sometimes you do want to tell them what a nightmare you are living.

To have a relatively peaceful, happy and loving Luke was wonderful. It is important to hang on to those positive times but it is also even more disappointing when the negative behaviour kicks in again. Human nature is wonderfully optimistic though. You live in hope. Still do!

We had been waiting for two years to see an occupational therapist, having been reliably informed that the waiting list was at least eighteen months and it was, reliably longer! An appointment came through for her to come to see us at the house. Luke was now nearly ten and still couldn't eat with a knife and fork or tie his shoelaces. A lovely lady came and spent a couple of hours with Luke, asking him questions and getting him to do various tests which he loved, not only because he had one to one attention, which he craves, but also because he was missing school. Luke concentrated with the help of the *Ritalin* but as soon as her tests were over, he lost interest in her entirely and shot off to do whatever his little brain was obsessed with at that particular stage of life.

She told me that Luke had been able to tie his shoelaces and use a knife and fork, albeit clumsily and had demonstrated those skills to her as soon as she told him that was why she was there.

Bearing in mind that we had been referred by our GP *two years* previously I still felt embarrassed that she had come to see us unnecessarily but she explained that the fact he could physically do those things but his brain wouldn't let him, (he only ever ate with his fingers) and also that she felt he had some significant language difficulty, meant that she would suggest in her report that he had some further testing for Aspergers Syndrome, a 'communication disorder'.

Ritalin didn't really work for us, as a family. When he was taking it Luke couldn't eat and he couldn't sleep and although he was calmer at school, by the time he came home the effects were wearing off and he became even more hyper before bedtime. Dr Murray prescribed Melatonin to try and regulate Luke's sleep patterns and that does work but we only used it as a last resort. No parent medicates their child willingly and Melatonin, although a natural hormone, is not registered in the UK for use on children. So we decided to take Luke off *Ritalin* during the school holidays and to be honest, there wasn't much to choose between a frantic Luke or a drugged Luke with side effects. I think, on balance, that it was a good thing to try it because it gave him an idea of how it felt to have some control over his impulsive behaviour. That in turn, improved his self-esteem. Which did bring us into a more positive place for a time. Luke hasn't taken *Ritalin* since. I wish I could say that it worked for us but it didn't. However I have met parents who swear by it and I am envious of them.

Jan's tip: It's a hard decision to take, to give your child a cocaine derivative, classified drug that alters behaviour and acts directly on the brain. I'm glad that we tried it for Luke's sake. Anything that helps is worth trying. *Ritalin* or *Methylphenidate* is not a wonder drug though. Its' long-term use hasn't been documented and for us, the side effects outweighed any benefits to Luke. It's worth trying if your child is hyperactive though because no one but the parent of a truly hyperactive child knows just how physically and emotionally exhausting it is to live with. Peter Hitchens from the Daily Mail take note please: - Don't talk about things you obviously know nothing about. Save your crusades for the politicians who want the attention, or come and live with Luke for a week. Actually, please come and live with Luke for a week. I could have a holiday doing your job.

Melatonin is the best thing we have found to help Luke get to sleep and stay asleep. He can't switch his brain off and yet he is so tired that he is like a bear with an awfully sore head. *Melatonin* doesn't knock him out, just relaxes him, in order to settle down for sleep and its' big bonus is that he doesn't wake up in the morning feeling any more drowsy and disorientated than usual. It helps to kick him back into a sleeping pattern if he can't get to sleep naturally.

Luke's tip: When I was on *Ritalin* I felt calmer and I liked that control. I felt more normal and I was much better at concentrating. I didn't chew my clothes or eat my books or scribble all the time at school. But I didn't really feel like me. Nothing tasted right, I couldn't get to sleep at night and I felt as though ants were crawling on my skin. Also, my eyes kept blinking by themselves and I got scared easily. I just didn't feel right. Everyone says that you should never take drugs and then people were saying I should take drugs. If you asked me though I would tell you to try it. It was really lovely for me to feel in control. I didn't understand until then what it felt like to be normal. It made me feel that other people could like me. When I am frantic even I don't like me. It is horrible when you want to stop but your brain won't let your body have a holiday. Even when I am ill or really tired I can't stop the messages from my brain which make me keep moving, jumping, talking and then I get very angry because I am fed up with myself, and very tired. Today I am like that and I have just smashed things, because it is the only way I can let the frustration out. Then I am upset because usually I smash something special. How dumb is that?

5/7/01. Tuffy's Diary (Wednesday)

So spank me! I bought a dead mouse into there presios home. I mean come on! The thing crawled on to me while I was snoozing. It could of killed me! I Just used self defence. Ok maybe I shouldent of dumomped the mammal on mums (now) white blood stained bed.

Of course when Ellie saw the mouse she... Blubered all over me!!! This time I was so wet and whinded I had to lye on the boyler for three hours. (After I scratched Ellies cheek) Mum and Dad where Mad! They even kicked Me!

All I did was walk of and give them the wink the hiss and a big tail whip. But for a big annoying absourlutely stuipid fact people have no idea what life is like; for cats!

Luke's handwriting whilst taking Ritalin.

10/9/02. Electricity ⚡

Electricity is a flow of electrons around a continuous conductive loop or a circuit. Electricity can be created in a number ow of ways, for example: solar energy uses the energy from the sun to create electricity; ~~hydro~~ tidal energy uses the energy in moving water such as the sea, ~~wind~~ wind energy uses the energy from the wind & hydro-electric is created from falling water. However it is most commonly created in small amounts by a m number of cells or ~~battery~~ Electricity can be used to power many home aplieros such as a television or dish washer as well as provide street lights across whole countries

Luke's handwriting over a year later without Ritalin

CHAPTER 9 LABELLING OF LUKE - ASPERGERS SYNDROME

So it was that I found myself back in the familiar surroundings of Dr Murray's treatment room, just before Christmas, this time without Luke, undergoing a three-hour diagnostic interview that would confirm whether he did have Aspergers Syndrome. At the end of the interview, Luke had graduated with honours from the school of autism. Because of the time of diagnosis, he collected the label of Aspergers Syndrome, but he could equally qualify for the high-functioning autism label because his symptoms were obviously there from infancy. I don't think that anyone who hasn't been there can comprehend what it feels like to hear the word **autism** in connection with your own child. ADHD as a label was ok. It explained Luke's behavioural difficulties; most people understood it and you had the hope that he would grow out of it. As a condition, it is a nightmare, but as a label it is acceptable. Autism, on the other hand, is a lifelong condition, and what exactly does it mean in terms of job expectancy, life expectancy, adult behaviour, understanding, etc etc? The only thing I really knew about it was the character *Raymond* that Dustin Hoffman played in the film *'Rain Man'*. So many questions but in all reality, very few answers. My mum said to me "No matter what labels he has, he is still Luke".

Aspergers Syndrome is thought of as a *mild* form of autism because the person can communicate, is of average or above intelligence and appears able to socialize. Well, in Luke's case I beg to differ. In our experience there is nothing mild about his autism. In some ways, it is harder to deal with than a more extreme form of autism because Luke looks normal and has a wicked command of the English language. But, and this is a big BUT his brain does not work in the same way as yours and mine. It processes information differently and he has great difficulty fitting in. He can very quickly 'fit out' and then people assume he is behaving badly by choice. Believe me, if he could choose to behave normally, he would.

I left Dr Murray's room with tears pricking at my eyes but as always, try and act calmly, professionally and save the tears for later. I don't remember what advice, if any, he gave me but I do remember that he had a medical student with him throughout the interview, a girl. She told me that she wasn't planning on having children herself after hearing what children like Luke meant to live with. I did ask myself then whether I would go back and do things differently had I known what could go wrong and I can't honestly say that I know the answer to that question on a bad day.

So a Happy Christmas. And a Happy Autistic New Year. Or an Autistic Happy New Year. Whatever.

We decided not to tell Luke that he had graduated with honours from the school of autism. We thought that his ADHD label was enough for him to live with at the time.

I was watching a programme called *Children Behaving Badly* on TV one evening, not long after Luke's diagnosis and Luke was in the playroom watching a video, his favourite of the moment. The playroom TV was linked to the main TV and at some point Luke's video had finished and my programme came on to his screen. He continued to watch, unknown to me, fascinated by this boy's behaviour which so closely matched his own. The boy was diagnosed with Aspergers Syndrome and the boy's mother was so shocked that she started to cry and I was crying too, the experience and shock of diagnosis mirroring our own recent experiences.

All of a sudden, a quiet little boy came into the room and sat next to me. (He looks smaller when he's quiet, he is usually larger than life.) In a very quiet voice he said "that's what I've got isn't it mummy? Aspergers Syndrome, that's exactly what's wrong with me too, isn't it?"

I had no idea until then that he had been watching anything other than his video and was so surprised that he had the insight to diagnose himself, aged just ten. He then checked my face to see if I was crying and was pleased to see that I was. He said that he would feel very cheated if the other boy's mum was upset and his mum wasn't. We talked a little before he lost interest and went off to play and that was the first time I realised just how insightful Luke is into his own condition.

He described himself as a person with many personalities. He said that he could understand why his friends found him confusing and likened it to visiting the zoo. "One day you will see a friendly, stripy zebra, the next a tall gentle giraffe" (can't see the resemblance myself - he doesn't do gentle, but these are Luke's words) "and then a snarling lion or a tiger pacing up and down looking cross and fierce and you don't know which animal you are going to find or what to expect and you may well get pounced on". Gareth Hill was one of Luke's friends at primary school and he was Luke's pouncing victim. Something about him compelled Luke to jump on him and squeeze him round the neck. He was very patient, resigned to his fate but eventually he had had enough. Sorry Gareth. He used to kiss you too, after strangulation. Luke's kiss of death!.

Olly is Luke's cousin and his uber-hero. Olly is four years older than Luke and now drives a blue mini, and is head boy of Bristol Cathedral School which makes him ultra cool too. He has always been a big influence in Luke's life and also on his behaviour. When Luke was younger and used to throw the most amazing tantrums, with much accompanying vocalization, Olly would say to him "nice singing practise old chap". The 'old chap' was Luke's favourite expression at the time, he loves formal language and uses it often. From then on we referred to Luke's tantrums as his 'singing practice'.

One Saturday, Luke was desperate to see Olly. He was struggling with friendships at school and just needed a familiar 'boy face' to relate to. On the way to Bristol, Luke talked to me. He said that in his dreams he is normal, although he doesn't really know what normal is. He said he would give anything to be like his friends, enjoying new experiences without either getting too scared and doing a runner or getting too excited and going over the top. He said he felt different under the skin.

Anyway we tracked Olly down to a barn dance on the outskirts of Bristol but when we got there, Luke went into another place in his head. He started hyperventilating, crying, shivering. All his senses were in overload. Too many people, smells, lights, too much noise and nothing familiar. Just panic. We had to go back home again and in the car Luke was sick, shivering one minute, hot the next, crouched on the floor, unable to put the seat belt on even though we were on the M4. He told me that he couldn't hear Olly's words, it was too noisy, and that Olly was speaking to him in face language only and he didn't know whether Olly was pleased to see him or cross with him for coming and he didn't understand this language and it scared him. Olly's familiar face was unreadable to Luke without being able to hear his words.

Then he told me about an incident that had happened at Cubs a few weeks before that explained what had gone wrong with his sense of self and security. They were putting on a play and he loves acting and being the centre of attention when he's pretending to be someone else. At the vital moment for him in the play, he tripped over and as he lay there, exposed as clumsy Luke, stupid Luke, the real Luke, not his character, he had started to cry with frustration and the other boys had laughed at him. He says that in that moment he knew that he was a social outcast and that was the loneliest he had ever felt. I asked him why he hadn't talked about it on the night but he said he had wanted to try and forget about it. He also said that he thought I would be dismissive, say something like "well, that's just you Luke, you're always clumsy," and disregard his feelings. I haven't been the world's best listener, he is right about that. I did think that I had to give out advice at that time but I have since realised that when he talks he just wants to be heard, listened to. Doesn't everyone?

Once Luke was diagnosed, nothing really changed apart from me. I felt so sad. I read *Tony Attwood's* book -*Aspergers Syndrome ;A Guide for Parents and Professionals* published by *Jessica Kingsley*, which was a good starting point from which to understand the label and its' implications. I went to hear Tony Attwood speak about a year and a half ago and he has first hand knowledge of his subject. He is funny, irreverent and very insightful, (as well as nice-looking). I wish that everyone who had contact with Luke could hear him describe the behaviour typical of the condition. Perhaps they would be less inclined to think that they could change him and be more accepting of who he is and how hard it is being him. I do find it very fascinating that these children with totally different backgrounds and genes have brains that react in the same programmed way, quite often, even down to the list of foods that they will/won't eat.

It was a frightening thing to re evaluate your ten-year-old son in the light of a lifelong condition. I am sad for Luke and what it means for him. His life will always be much harder to live than mine and understanding his struggles doesn't change them for him. In some ways it has made it harder to help him.

Luke however, went off to find a machine that prints business cards. He designed himself one with a red car, his address, phone numbers and email address. His title read **LUKE DICKER, child with Aspergers Syndrome and ADHD**. They're the letters after his name and he's got them so he decided to use them. My uncle Alan is a professor and has lots of letters after his name that Luke finds very impressive so he decided to follow suit. It has been a very good way for him to introduce himself in a realistic but positive way. Luke usually has an answer up his sleeve for any given situation and he is uncannily accurate at times with his straight-line thinking.

Jan's tip: Reading the right book once Luke was diagnosed was really helpful although, to be honest, I haven't read that much about autism because when I get any time away from Luke I want to switch off and grab a little bit of a real life and when I am with Luke he is all consuming. Also, I have been writing this book in my head as a way of making some sense of it all. The *National Autistic Society* have a comprehensive list of relevant books and of course *The Curious Incident of the dog in the Night Time* by *Mark Haddon* needs no recommending. Abbi and some of her friends have read it and it has given them some empathy for Luke's unusual way of thinking.

Luke's Tip: it was a big relief for me to know that I had another label which explained my confusion and my difference. I knew I was different under the skin and I felt really lonely. When I knew that my loneliness had a name it made such a difference. I tell people that I have Aspergers Syndrome. It explains why I behave differently sometimes. Of course there are the cynics who say that I use it as an excuse for my behaviour. Blah, blah, blah. There are lots of famous people who are meant to have it and they are like me, inventive and unusual. My mum says Peter Sellers sounds like he had it and *Mr. Bean* definitely has it, the character, that is. I want to tell you who else has it but my mum says we can't. Write to me, enclosing a cheque and I'll tell you, confidentially, of course. You'll be surprised! Or maybe not. I can find another person with Aspergers Syndrome a mile away. I always do on holiday. Maybe we smell different! Last time we went to Centerparcs just for the day I found a girl with ADHD and Aspergers Syndrome as soon as we went in to the pool area. Her name is Cathy and we got on brilliantly and we text each other although, because I keep smashing my phone, I haven't done that recently.

Abbi's tip: reading *The Curious incident of the dog in the night time* helped me to understand why Luke behaves the way he does. I did feel very sorry for him when I realised how his brain is so different to mine. Most people think that everyone thinks like them but Luke has had to try and understand that he is different. He is trying really hard to like different foods and to understand a point of view. When things aren't going his way and I look into his eyes he sometimes looks really lost, like he just doesn't get it and I guess he doesn't.

CHAPTER 10 SIBLINGS - ABBI'S CHAPTER

Abbi's poem about Luke.

I'm straight like beams of sunlight shining through the clouds

But my light looks different from yours

It's just not the same

I can't even pretend it's a game

And that is why you won't find any curves or bends in me

Otherwise I wouldn't take things so literally.

Abbi has grown up with Luke. She knows no other life and yet it has been really tough for her at times. She has to watch him, be very wary of him, guard her possessions against him and although she is the youngest, continually take responsibility for him. She has the sweetest personality but nowadays, she has the quickest wit and she does not suffer fools gladly.

Boys hold no mystery, no intrigue for her after Luke and she prefers horses. Her cousin Lisa was killed in a car accident aged just 21years and she also loved horses. They would have loved to ride out together. The boy who was driving the car that smashed into Lisa's car on her way to work had been smoking cannabis. He was driving like an idiot and he killed Lisa and died himself after three painful weeks of fighting for his life. They were friends too and he obviously didn't have any idea of consequences either. What a terrible tragic waste of life. Lisa was an only child and her mum and dad had their grandchildren taken away from them in that puff of a joint. The coroner recorded a verdict of unlawful killing at her inquest but that didn't bring her back. Cannabis is a killer in our family. If Luke were to smoke it when he is older, he would probably become psychotic. His brain is not wired up for substances and he doesn't need any extra stimuli. We don't protect the more vulnerable members in our society with liberalism and we all pay the price then.

Luke has always been violent in his anger. He will attack, smash and hit anything in close range so I try to make sure that Abbi isn't within hitting range. My senses are always primed for trouble, nerves jangling and ears swiveling. When he is anxious and edgy he is always dangerous and those moments come out of nowhere sometimes.

I wrote this after just another Sunday afternoon at **'The Edge'**.

So you think that you can sit there in judgment, knowing what it feels like to be in my shoes? Well, what would you do as a mother when you walk into the playroom on a Sunday afternoon and your eldest child is hitting your youngest child on the head with a hammer. You look at her face and she is in fear of her life. Too afraid to cry. Not from a stranger, but from her eleven year old brother. It's not that simple. He suffers from Aspergers Syndrome and *suffers* is the word here. Don't let anyone tell you it is the mild form of autism. It is a heartless form of autism because he knows that he is different and yet is powerless to control his behaviour. He is so sorry and remorseful after his outbursts but that doesn't take away the effects of his temper for him or for us.

And what of her? Does she deserve to live in fear because he has this illness that is becoming so common yet is still so misunderstood?

And what of us, the parents? How do you deal with this behaviour when your protective instincts for her make you want to kill him? And who is there for you when you cry with guilt that you weren't there to protect her because you were being the mum and putting the vegetables on to cook? Vegetables that he can't or won't eat anyway because they are the wrong shape, texture, colour, smell.

Read the books, they tell you in black and white what it is like to have a child with Aspergers Syndrome but they don't tell you in glorious colour how red the blood is as it pumps out of your child's head on a Sunday afternoon.

What do you do when he is damaged and she is your baby and you've had enough?

Let me tell you that we have asked for help. We are proud and self-sufficient but I have begged for help. Not asking for money, although the irony is that we'd probably get that, but asking for things that you would think were available in the 21st century. Things like help at school in the form of an Educational Statement of special needs, help from Social Services. Specialist help - behavioural therapy, anger management, respite care, any kind of help. We want help and we need it now. Why should we have to wait two years for medical appointments? I have a file this thick of letters that I have written in my quest for help. When I was a little girl we used to be asked to write essays at school imagining what life would be like in the 21st century and I imagined wonderful things, exciting things, happy things. I thought that progress was assured. Little did I think I would spend my life in fear of my son's moods, planning how to protect my daughter from him, without any help whatsoever from the society which has invented a global language and mobile phones, can send men into space and puts speed cameras all along our stretch of the M4.

I felt such anger when I saw her little face, the tears streaming down her soft cheeks, her mouth open in a silent cry for help that all reason left me. She's my baby, the youngest and so little still. I took the hammer from him and I passed it to her and I held him down and told her to hit him just once to show him what it felt like to be held down and hit on the head with a hammer. She hit him alright, a solid smashing blow that repaid him for all the other Sunday, Monday, Tuesday, Wednesday, Thursday, Friday and Saturday morning, afternoon and evenings hurts of her little life.

His head burst open in a fountain of red blood and he howled like an animal and took off in panic as his nervous system registered the shock and hurt in the way that an Asperger's child does. The blood spurted all over the wooden floor and up the stairs as he ran blindly, banging at his head to try and stop the pain, his fight or flight mechanism well and truly primed.

He had a hole in his head that my friend Bernadette, a nurse, dressed for us and that took a few days to heal but because he sees things in black and white he accepted that he hit, he got hit. Fact. It was a lesson he took on board and he learns only from extremes.

Luke apologized to Abbi when he came back from Bernadette's. He said that he deserved his hole in the head and that he was very sorry for hurting her and frightening her. He resents her loveliness and takes his anger out on her readily but he does love her in his own way. Abbi did not take the apology readily, she was very shocked at the strength of her own reaction, as I was (what kind of mother am I?) and she was still in shock at all the blood and drama.

A few days later, when the shock of the day was beginning to wear off for Abbi, she said to Luke "I know what I'm going to call you from now on, hammer head". Luke loved that. He has always loved sharks, he relates better to animals and he liked the humour that implied resolution, a way forward, forgiveness.

One really good thing about Luke is that he will always say sorry. He may not be able to control his impulsive behaviour, he can't calculate the consequences of what he does, he doesn't often understand what drove him to that extreme so suddenly, ferociously but what he does understand is saying sorry. He always does and it tugs at my heart every time. He has no pride in saying it, just a genuine sadness and remorsefulness that he has once again upset the equilibrium. A lot of autistic children don't say sorry, they see no reason to. I am very glad that Luke does, it gives us a way forward. The Lord's Prayer says 'Forgive us our sins as we forgive one another'. Forgiveness is the only way forward for a child like Luke. Hanging onto today's mistakes, no matter how big they are, turns them into tomorrow's resentments. The world would be a better place if we could all say sorry like Luke and expect to draw a line under it, to be forgiven.

Siblings of autistic children are in their shadow. Luke is so demanding and Abbi has had to grow up very quickly. She has been denied a normal childhood in many ways. She is actually a carer. This is a 2way street. She is empathic and kind, has a great sense of humour and underplays, rather than overplays a situation. However, she has had to develop a tough exterior because she lives with the stress of anger being only a fist away from her face or her bedroom or her possessions. She tries to comfort me when I am stressed out and is very protective of me, phoning for help when she knows we need it, if Luke is being very violent towards me. She has the phone number of our local police in her mobile and she has used it. I have made sure that her teachers at school understand what life is like for her. There have been times when girls at school have really upset her. She is older than her years and expects a lot of friendship, including loyalty, listening and discretion because she possesses those qualities. When her friends behave like the little girls they are, she can be left out because she can't deal with all the make friends, break friends stuff. However, she does have some good family friends, most of them older than her, Claire Johnson in our village and her cousin Heidi particularly have been very supportive and she has needed that.

Luke's autism means that quite often he can't go out and face the world because he doesn't feel like seeing people on his anxious days. This has meant that Abbi has been denied many normal family times. Only we really know that side of Luke because you only get to see him when he is able to face the world and he may be excitable, loud and over the top or rarely, relatively ok. Abbi and I know the true Luke, the sad and scared Luke, the very angry and frightening Luke, the aggressive and smashing Luke. We live with all the versions and have to cope with whatever the day or the moment brings. *The only predictable thing about Luke is his unpredictability.*

It is hard for me but for her it is exacerbated by the sibling relationship and she longs for some peace and quiet. The absolute rule is and always has been that you don't hit a girl. However our reality is that Luke has, often and hard. So one day, after he came out of school angry and upset, he started throwing stones at Abbi. I realised that we needed to get home to deal with whatever was about to erupt and I picked her up and ran home with her. Luke followed, throwing stones at us and the ones that hit, hurt. Once we got home my instincts took over. I was hurting and mad, but at some deeper level I also realised that Luke had to have some sort of respect for us. No matter how upset he was he couldn't take his anger out on us like that so I told him to go to his bedroom. Paul had put a lock on the outside of his bedroom door at this point so that when he was really violent I could lock him in there until he had worn himself out, rather than attack Abbi or me. This felt barbaric but was really the only way to save him from the consequences of his frustration. (He had smashed every piece of furniture in his room that was smashable during these lock-ins. Better that than Abbi.) Well, as usual he refused and he started to fight me. He punched me so I pinned him down, held him on the floor and boy was he mad. He is so strong, but my anger and weight combined were stronger. I punched him in the ribs, hard and sure because he had to know that I was strong. I was acting on instinct, not just anger and that was the message he needed, as he later explained to me. His brain says that if he is the dominant male he will take control. If he is subdued by force then he has to respect that dominance. Truly, that is his logic. Like the animal kingdom, it's that basic! Every so often, I have had to reprove my physical strength to Luke again so that he knows who is in control. There is a safety for children in knowing that adults rule the world. Well, Luke needs to know who rules his world, if only for Abbi's sake. The problem here is that he is fast becoming stronger than me. (He has been a misogynist almost from birth and interestingly, Tony Attwood's book bears this out as a recognizable trait of AS! In fact I think that autism in him is like the extreme form of male behaviour, caveman style.)

Back to that punch in the ribs. It hurt him enough to make him cry. Even as a baby Luke didn't shed tears. He hardly ever does. He makes the sound of crying. His face screws up but usually no tears fall. Well that punch made him shed tears and I can't begin to tell you how utterly sad I felt when I looked at him crying real tears, yet unable to accept a cuddle and show any emotion other than anger. What must it feel like to be him? I swore then that I would help him, be there for him, no matter what, and I have. Luke explained to me that it is because he trusts me and Abbi to love him always that he can show us his worst behaviour. I think that is what you call a backhanded compliment! It doesn't mean that we have to accept his awful behaviour and it does mean that we have to challenge him, try and change him where possible, but we also have to accept him for who he is and above all, love him when his behaviour is totally unlovable. That is the challenge.

Luke's aggression has been, for me, one of the hardest things to deal with. I am naturally a peacemaker; I hate confrontation and anger and am very frightened of violence. I have had to fight Luke off, my own child, as I would do a man - once on the stairs as he was trying to push me down them and I was fighting, literally, to stay in one place. I have been covered in bruises, have been bitten and punched and menaced in my own home. Luke has told me that he wants to kill me, he hates me because he loves me, hates the strong emotional attachment to me and his ongoing need of me. I, on the other hand, feel so protective of Abbi that I have felt, at times, like killing Luke when he has hurt her.

Abbi and I are emotional giants. We live with the hurt, confusion, damage, embarrassment and exhaustion of Luke's behaviour and yet we love and understand him and we can't take his behaviour personally. For me, that just about works for three out of four weeks but hormones play a part too. For Abbi, she is absolutely brilliant at coping and I am full of admiration for her. She will be an exceptional adult. She is an exceptional child and she deserves a medal.

Jan's tip: Luke needs his behaviour dealt with unemotionally. This is almost impossible for a mum to do and it is why he needs specialist help. It is one of the reasons that I am writing this book because there isn't the help out there for us, three years after our hammerhead Sunday afternoon, and we have had to do this alone. I hope that by telling Luke's story, by telling it like it is, that we will help you to get help if you need it. I have been at breaking point, my marriage didn't survive and even my parents haven't been able to cope with the reality of Luke. It is the loneliest path and yet Luke is worth fighting for. If I don't fight for him, (as well as fight him!) then what kind of mum am I?

Luke's tip: the thing that has helped me to understand my tantrums most is seeing a video of my behaviour. My dad was videoing me opening my presents one Christmas and I opened a video of Aladdin that my auntie Maggie had bought me. I didn't like Aladdin at the time, I was scared of it for some reason and when I saw the present I threw it across the room and started to throw a tantrum. Another time we were skiing and I fell over as I came off a jump. Again my dad was videoing me. I took off my skies, threw them as far as I could (luckily I didn't hit anyone) and stamped off in a temper. When I saw how funny my behaviour looked to other people, it made me realise how dramatic I am and it was like watching a cartoon character.

When I am really angry, I need the person controlling me to stand up to me but not to react to my anger. Emotion makes me even madder and my mum is the wrong person to deal with me because she gets upset. If I am out of control I really need to be left alone but that is impossible because I cause so much damage with my temper. I am getting better now and I don't lose my temper anywhere near as often as I used to but I hate myself afterwards and want to kill myself. I do love my mum and my sister very much and I hope they know that.

Abbi's tip: I try to ignore Luke's aggressive behaviour until it reaches the point where I am going to get hurt. If Luke breaks my things then I sometimes break something of his, usually an old toy that he has forgotten about, which won't make him too upset but it helps to relieve my anger and shows him what it feels like too.

I need a break from Luke and I really need to have places where I can go to escape from him.

I hate it when he hurts my mum and I hate it when she loses it with him. I long for peace and quiet and I long for a normal life but I have to stand up for myself. Luke is getting better in some ways because he now has more respect for us but we have had to fight to get it. He hit my mum to the floor this week and then punched her on the back of the head twice and I am the only person there to help her.

I don't like those people who think that you can change Luke. They have no idea how hard it is to live with him and how hard me and my mum work, all the time, to teach him, show him, help him and still have a life of our own. My friends have no idea how lucky they are to know what comes next. With my brother I never know how it is going to be but I don't hate him any more. As I grow up I feel more sorry for him because I know how desperate he is to be normal and to be popular.

CHAPTER 11 FRIEND OR FOE?

Luke's behaviour *is* his disability. That is the problem. The part of his brain that controls certain aspects of behaviour is damaged. It doesn't work, it won't work. If your legs don't work you use crutches or a wheelchair. Would you tell someone in a wheelchair whose legs were damaged at birth, "Pull yourself together. Get up and walk. You can choose to do it if you really want to"? No, you wouldn't because that would be cruel. Well, on that basis, lots of people have been cruel to Luke in his lifetime and the people who should understand have often been the worst offenders. Luke needs the equivalent of a wheelchair for his brain.

Most of us need control. We feel best about ourselves when we can, at least influence and at best control, our immediate environment. Control is the thing that slips away when I am with Luke. He has such a blueprint of what will and won't happen, when, how and where. It is the most determined and tunnel-visioned view of life and it is his reality. No matter patience, understanding, cajoling, placating, distracting. Nothing works. Right from the age of two there was no tactic known to man or dog that could or would make any difference to his implacable mindset.

Of course every man and his dog has the answer. "Give him to me for a week and I'll sort him out." Yeah, right, it's a lifetime's job. Or the more subtle approach, but nonetheless deadly, "if I were you I would just ignore him, he'll soon get fed up". If only. Do they think I haven't tried ignoring, tried everything? (Including head-butting him once in sheer and utter frustration.) The hardest thing, as Luke's mum, has been to understand at an instinctive level that his behaviour was and is a part of him. And then to juggle that understanding with the confusion, damage and embarrassment that his behaviour presents both to him and us, all on a few hours sleep and with next to no professional help whatsoever in our daily lives.

So if you are reading this chapter and you know someone in my shoes, please be gentle with them. Listen to them and don't try and give them solutions. Understand that tears are close companions and feel their exhaustion. Be very glad that you can step away and give words of encouragement whilst standing close. Most of all distract them. Buy them some flowers. Help them laugh, feel funny and human again. That is a fine gift, to encourage another person on their journey.

I can't mention all the people who have been there for us although I would love to. I hope they know who they are. There are two groups really, our friends and family members who have been there through thick and thin and the very few professionals who we have contact with.

I also, for diplomatic reasons, can't mention those people who have been judgmental or hurtful in their attitude to Luke although I would like to! My guess is that they won't even pick this book up because they think they know it all already!

Falling right in the middle though is my friend Sue. Her son Adam has Aspergers Syndrome and she runs the North Wiltshire Autistic Support Group. When Luke was finally given his AS label, someone recommended the support group to me. That was the last place I intended to park my backside, I can tell you. Not for me the sadness of saying, "my name is Jan and I have an autistic son". I really couldn't accept the label and I didn't want to meet a load of people as sad as I felt right then. No, denial was the best policy! However God has always got the handle on me. He knows I can't say no to someone else's need and another mum in our village who couldn't drive asked me to take her to the next meeting. So of course I said yes and in so doing, discovered one of my best friends. (I always tell the children to try and keep an open mind because you might find the thing you really love and how will you know, unless you try it? I should take my own advice!)

As soon as I met Sue we formed an instant bond. She is a nurse, calm and very funny in a self-deprecating way, all wrapped up in a gentle welsh lilt. We are a similar age. We have our boys and our hormones in common and we belong to a different family. One that we wouldn't choose to belong to, but one that understands, really understands and the relief is enormous. Feelings held in come tumbling out, confessions fly, tears fall and laughter is ever present. Laughter is the healer, especially when you discover that our boys destroy remote controls. What button is it that pushes their brains to destroy remote controls, along with every other gadget too?

The support group provides access to any available (in our dreams!) specialist help and shared experiences. It is a lifeline and there I meet Louise who has three boys all on the autistic spectrum. Her life is a fight to get any kind of help. How can that be ok when she has no energy left to fight for anything when looking after three boys, let alone three autistic boys? Autism is not classed as mental illness so it falls outside any kind of category. No box, no tick, no resources. So many children are being diagnosed now; latest statistics suggest 1 in 110 children, that it should be a category all on its own. Incidentally, there are five boys diagnosed to every one girl.

I meet Wendy, another welsh girl and we discover that our boys both have a compulsion to hang out of the car window, even on the motorway. We both know the impossibility of driving on the M4 with our boys, who have to obey their strong instinct, hanging so far out of the window that they defy gravity. We both know how impossible it is to stop them and how impossible it is to concentrate properly on driving when they are in the car. Luke climbed out of the sunroof once when we were stuck on the M4 in a traffic jam for three hours and he wouldn't get back into the car. We had just come from the hospital, having had the plaster removed from his 2nd broken arm. He had been waiting, one way and another, all day and he couldn't stand it any longer. I had no tactics left to get him back into the car and so, just as the traffic had finally started to move again, we were going nowhere because Luke was on the roof. That reinforced the point that with Luke, the unexpected is a disaster waiting to happen and explains why even a simple outing can turn into an emotional minefield. Guilt is ever present and that day I felt so guilty for not having taken anything for Luke to do, or eat and drink, although we were only travelling from Junction 17 to Junction 16, in theory a twenty minute journey, and never mind that my bladder had nearly burst by the time we got home. Always go prepared for the unexpected is the moral of the story and so we rarely do impromptu, sadly, because I love being impulsive.

Cathy was my secretary back in the earliest days of banking, although she would be the first to admit that her secretarial skills were far below her personality value. She is tall, vibrant and makes things happen. We were as different as it is possible for two people to be, physically, politically and in our personalities and yet we connected. I remember her cooking us fried eggs in the middle of the night, probably all we could afford back then, as we read each other our poetry. When she left to work in an old people's home and later to train as a psychiatric nurse we lost touch for about ten years, although I never forgot her.

At my first antenatal class when I was pregnant with Luke, in walked this tall and unforgettable figure whose first baby was due, amazingly, on the same day as mine and our friendship resumed. We shared the remainder of our pregnancies and although Ellie was born two days later than Luke, we were in adjoining rooms at the same hospital. Ellie and Luke are both 'Child of the 90's' children. Ellie was a big baby and had to be delivered by forceps. So Cathy and I shared the agonies of our first wee after childbirth and much more. Cathy's husband Colin is a doctor but that didn't stop the nurses giving us some serious tellings off for leaving our babies in their plastic cots and going off for a fag and a natter. Neither of us could walk properly or sit down with any degree of ease and to watch the other one hobbling around made us crack up. It made the aftermath of giving birth a lovely time of shared experiences.

When Luke was ill, our friendship was torn apart for a while. Cathy felt abandoned, particularly because Ellie was such an unhappy baby, probably due to her birth experience. (Cranial osteopathy would probably have helped if Cathy had known about it then.) I was unaware of anything except the shock of Luke being so ill. I lived in the goldfish bowl existence of the hospital and so, for a while, our lives took different paths but we resumed our friendship once Luke was finally out of hospital and it is Cathy who gave me the impetus to write this book. She talked it through with me and gave me the excitement of thinking that anything is possible if you are passionate about it. That's her philosophy and she always inspires me to better things. She gets up at 6am every morning to practise the guitar, having taught herself to play, for goodness sake. Her twin girls, Alice and Emily were born five weeks after Abbi, they are great friends, and our families have had many memorable holidays together. They all love Luke, having seen the best and the worst of him. They love his energy, as Cathy is a very energetic person and they feel free to tell him if he is being antisocial or rude or both but most importantly, he knows that they really do accept him as he is. One of Luke's more antisocial habits is to snort, loud and long and he isn't really aware of doing it. Cathy and my sister Libbi take him to task for it and he does try and stop it for them, out of respect. Cathy is now a well known (and brilliant) sculptor and musician. She has five brothers and is totally fascinating. Her friendship is fact, tried and tested, strong and loyal and as we have grown older our politics and personalities have mellowed too and we are not as different now. Anyway, our differences have never come between us. If anything they have provided the spark between us.

We don't have the emotional energy for part time supporters. You are either for us or against us. We can criticise Luke but woe betide anyone else who thinks they can form a judgment based on first impressions. Elliott and James are Luke's firm friends. They can only tolerate so much of him at any given time and they don't always understand his need to withdraw into his own world, or his pedantic and forthright language, or his seemingly arrogant and bossy manner. They have seen him with a knife against his wrists - sad and depressed, angry and abusive, in fact they have seen more of Luke than most people will ever get to and yet they come back for more. Those are friends, true friends and you are very blessed if you find friends like that, no matter your age, colour, religion or disability. They protect Luke loyally and fiercely against the rest of the world.

My friends Bernadette and Kyla are my lifesavers. They are there through thick and thin, through tears and laughter, through every part of life. Three is a magic number for us. We are a triangle and we have lived through so much. They have both dealt with big crisis in their lives too. Kyla's youngest son Ryan has just completed three years of chemotherapy treatment for leukaemia and he is the bravest boy. Bernadette nurses hospice patients and death is a fact of life for her. Our friendship has been forged on the anvil of tears and held together by Kyla's optimism and Bernadette's determination. We have a bond that is unique and although they are ten years younger than me, they are such wise women. Women are the sisterhood that makes the world go round. We are the keepers of a nation's morals and emotions and woe betide society if us women give up on life and love.

I have three sisters and one brother (who I adore) and I used to say that I had a sister for every occasion. It becomes more difficult to stay in touch now that geography and children come between us and they have all, in their own ways, had problems coping with the effects of Luke's behaviour on me.

My sister Libbi is my best friend. She was at Abbi's birth and I reciprocated at the birth of her son Barnaby. She is fiercely protective of me, always has been and she knows how sensitive I am to criticism, especially in my parenting of Luke, when it is unjustified or down to misunderstanding. It would be impossible to imagine, unless you have been this close, the effort that goes into being his mum and the emotional cost, all for little or no discernable rewards in the conventional sense.

Don't get me wrong, we all need constructive criticism but that is rare in our experience. Criticism should never be handed out uninvited. That is insensitivity in the extreme. It is also a judgment and it hurts. A smile is best of all. When in doubt, say nought. Least said, soonest mended. You need to wear someone else's shoes, share their blisters even, before you can tell them the path to tread.

My sister Fran is a GP and used to tell me to take each stage of Luke's behaviour as just that, a phase he was going through. It helped to think that it would pass and we could move on eventually and, with her experience, I knew she was right. Even when Luke was still wetting the bed at night, age nine, she convinced me that it would sort itself out and one wonderful morning, he was dry and has been ever since. If I had taken it on board as a worry, Luke would have taken it on board too. He is sensitive to my feelings in a strange, primeval way, (he knows when my period is due before I do) and he has enough to worry about as it is. Damage limitation.

Maggie is my younger sister and we worked in the City at the same time although she used to earn more money than me and we had many a fun-filled lunch at Balls Brothers' wine bar, in the days before children. She is petite and her husband Al is six feet five and Luke loves that fact. Uncle Al used to be his height measurement for everything. "Is that house as tall as Uncle Al?" he would ask and six feet five was his point of reference. Their house is a beautiful, welcoming place of fun and food and her two boys Marc and Louis have loved Luke's energy, although he can be overwhelming after a while as he gets very over-excited around his cousins.

Wendy is my life-friend and she has come and taken care of Luke when I needed to spend a couple of nights in hospital and she gave up two days lucrative pay as a consultant to do so. She bribed him with a ride home in her BMW convertible if he went to school and didn't bat an eyelid at his peculiar ways and habits. She didn't react when he lost his temper with me on my return from hospital because I was sitting on the sofa where he likes to sit, even though I looked (and felt) like I was dying at the time! We always have time for each other, even if only by text some days and we share a friendship that goes way beyond, thanks in part to Luke. Incidentally, Luke doesn't really notice what a person's face looks like. He told me he only recognises someone once they have talked to him and he knows what the person looks like on the inside. Their facial features appear to be a blank to him. I wonder if it is the equivalent to when I was in Hong Kong and saw loads of Chinese faces coming towards me on the subway which all looked exactly the same?

The Johnsons are family friends from our village and we have many shared memories of fun-filled evenings and special times. They have also seen the best and the worst of Luke's behaviour and have loved him throughout. Alan has given Luke a man's perspective when he has needed it and Elaine and I have shared many a life experience, sometimes over a bottle of wine, and often accompanied by tears but much laughter too. We have honesty as our basis for friendship and it shows. Their children Claire and Rory have patiently obeyed Luke's commands and spent long and happy summer evenings dressing up and living out his latest obsession with him. I like to think that Luke has added to their childhoods too, with his unusual zest for life and vivid imagination. He has persuaded them to dress up and be childlike long after it is age appropriate! We were there last night for supper, they are wonderful hosts and they had bought me a set of dragonfly lights for my garden, a kindness that moved me to tears. God's love comes to us in the form of such kindness and just at the right moment too.

There is the other side of the equation too, those who dislike Luke, find him too difficult or too disruptive or too everything and they have put us at arm's length. That is an incredibly painful side of being Luke's mum because how can they know how hard we work to get the best from him and how easily a critical spirit destroys all that hard work. He is sensitive to that and can bring out the best and the worst in people. I have found him to be an incredible test of character, like litmus paper and he is accurate to the same degree!

Even my father has really struggled to cope with Luke's behaviour. Before he was diagnosed, dad used to think that he was poorly disciplined and badly behaved, along with the majority of other people, I suspect. A lot of people still think that Luke's behaviour can be controlled. That misses the point entirely. Luke has to be given control of his own behaviour and it is a tortuous process. His brain has to use the intelligent part to restrain and re-train his impulsive and emotive behaviour and it is still very much a work in progress.

I am sitting on the stair

The very bottom stair

Crying

Sobbing

Emotionally out of sorts

A woman thing

What else is there to do?

No sleep, no sense of peace

Just the mayhem that drags us all in its' wake

This is the reality of autism

It hurts, it really hurts

This autism thing

It turns sane people into shells

Fine on the outside

But empty as blank paper on the inside

Broken dreams

Reality just out of reach

Almost within grasp and then slipping off into a distant memory

I am sitting on the stair

The very bottom stair

Crying

Tears and mascara mingling in smoky rivulets down my cheeks

And this little figure comes to find me

He tips his head curiously

Then he begins to smile

"O Mummy" he says, "you have melted chocolate on your face"

And he cups my face in his two little hands

And starts to lick away the tears

And the truth is fine and funny again, for now.

74

I wrote that one day, a lifetime of hurts ago, when we had been at my parents' home for a family gathering and as usual, Luke's behaviour had embarrassed himself and us. We had come away with the weight of disapproval settling around us like a grey cloud after the sunshine and the despair of our reality had made me sit on the bottom stair and cry as soon as we got inside the front door. I ask God to take each tear shed as a prayer for Luke and then it doesn't feel so pointless. Luke doesn't see tears, or understand them. He still doesn't. But this day he came to me, cupped my face in his hands and really did lick the tears away, unaware as far as I know that I was crying. It was one of those magical moments that the mum of an autistic child never, ever takes for granted. You might wait a long time for another such moment.

Jan's tip: I really, really wish that I could take my own advice here but being a mum is the hardest job in the world anyway. Let alone being the mum of a child like Luke and trying to juggle his demanding needs against those of your other children, your own and other people's. *Try to develop a thick skin* and not mind that other people don't, won't understand. You can't even begin to fight each battle in the bid to win the war. Identify those inner circle friends who you know love you and support you unconditionally. Take care of yourself. You are the key to your child because if you falter, the whole family goes with you. Each smile, word of encouragement, kind gesture or friendly touch is called a stroke. Psychologists say that each person needs fifty strokes a day to feel fulfilled! On the days when Luke is angry and aggressive and unable to leave the house, we have no contact with anyone else. Support groups and carers support groups exist to help and can put you in touch with relevant organisations.

The North Wilts Autistic Support group told me about claiming disability benefit for Luke and a carers allowance for me, (I had no idea that it was even available) and with form filling. I didn't think of myself as a carer, just a mum whose whole life was taken over with the parenting of my boy. The forms are a big job and you have to put the worst-case scenario even though some days are better than others and some nights you sleep and some you don't. Luke is so unpredictable that if you based his form on one day he wouldn't qualify and on the next he would be classed as severely disabled, so take the worst day as the base line because that is the reality.

Worst days happen for us and, unlike the weather, we get no warning of the storms ahead.

When a child is diagnosed, ideally the Consultant making the diagnosis would have an information pack to hand you, with relevant organizations, benefits available, telephone numbers for emergencies and other resources listed. Ideally. That would have helped a lot. I think, in the same way as getting treatment on the NHS, that where you live is a lottery in terms of the help you get. Our county of Wiltshire is probably one of the worst in terms of resources for families like us, or should I say the lack of them.

Luke's tip: because I only 'do' excited or angry, and not much in between, the friends that I have are my true friends, but even they get fed up with me. I take offence easily and bear a grudge and then I am in a terrible mood with them. I always say sorry afterwards though. Also, because I am obsessive I get like that with my friends, I talk too much and follow them round very closely - my friend James used to say, "Stop hounding me Luke". I can give them a headache with my constant talking. So I am learning now to give them space, to try and back off and if Elliott is at my house, which he often is, I go to my bedroom at regular intervals to give him a break from me. That is me at my most sensitive and even I am impressed.

On my bad days though I can't see anyone and I stay in my bedroom if someone is in our house and I get really mad if they try and see me. I have days when it is too hard to be Luke and I have to have time off from being me. So I dress up and become someone else and it gives me a break from myself. I get on my own nerves so I understand that I get on other people's nerves!

It is very lonely being me though and I have days when I am so lonely that I would rather be dead. Those are the days that no one can touch me or speak to me and I hate those days. They come for no reason and I don't know when they are coming. Usually I get a headache and am sick on those days too because nothing tastes right and my tummy hurts as well as my head.

I go inside my head then and I line my cars up or my 'Brittains' tractors and I make a world that I can control which doesn't include people because you can't control other people, although I do try to. Not because I want to control their minds but because I want them to be predictable and I need to know what is going to happen next.

CHAPTER 12 PROFESSIONALS - JUST THE FEW

Our MP James Gray was doing the bible reading at our village church one Sunday and Luke was unusually present. It was impossible then for him to sit still for an hour and that is still pretty much true today. He has climbed over pews, built towers of the prayer kneelers, stood on pews, climbed on the pillars, run away, eaten the hymn book pages, you name it, he's done it but everyone knows him and most people makes allowances for him.

However, at the end of this service Luke went and introduced himself to James Gray. He must have made a good impression because he got invited along for a personal guided tour of the House of Lords and the House of Commons. We got to go too, along with Luke's real life hero and cousin Olly and Olly's sister Heidi. It was a wonderful experience and Luke rose to the occasion, proud and pleased with himself as he had every right to be. He loved seeing the Queen's toilet, an original Crapper, in the House of Lords. James Gray took every care of us, even down to taking us onto the roof of the House of Commons and we all stood under Big Ben as it chimed eleven am. We were then admitted to the visitor's gallery after lunch and heard James Gray ask a question of Alistair Darling, then Minister for Transport about the stretch of M4 in our county of Wiltshire. His reply couldn't even be called an answer, it was pure, unadulterated waffle and when James looked up at Luke, who was hanging on every word, and gave him a conspiratorial wink, I felt so proud of my boy that my heart nearly burst. It gave him street cred in abundance with his cousins too.

Luke lobbied James Gray in the lobby, asking him to provide a playground for our village and he did try, coming to Parish council meetings and encouraging local efforts to raise money. The fact that it didn't happen wasn't for the want of trying, more to do with resistance to change locally. James writes a weekly column in the local *Gazette and Herald* newspaper and he kindly included a mention of our visit the following week.

Since then James Gray has been to tea at **'The Edge'**, again courtesy of Luke's invitation, and he has been very supportive of our situation. He has just written another letter to the Director for Education in Wiltshire on our behalf and he came to a meeting of the North Wilts Support Group to hear first hand what struggles we *all* have with the education of our autistic children. Just to know that he cares and uses his voice on our behalf is so important.

Our GP has also been very supportive. Luke's condition means that there are associated problems with his general health and our GP, Dr John Harrison, has been interested enough to take Luke and us on board. He recognises the stress that Luke's condition puts on the whole family and he has also written to the Local Education Authority on our behalf at least twice. When we have an appointment he always gives us as much time as we need and is very sensitive to Luke's dislike of being touched and his hyperactive behaviour. He also wrote us a letter; he has given me permission to reproduce it at the end of this chapter, which has been invaluable. When we first registered with the surgery we used to see whichever doctor was available. However, we realised that some doctors were more, others less, understanding and it is difficult to keep explaining Luke in a few minutes. He is too complicated and his medical file is that thick! Dr Harrison is in demand so we quite often have to wait a few days to see him but it is worth it. It is so much better to have that personal contact, to feel that you are known and understood and cared about and that goes for everyone, not just us.

Our dentist is another constant figure in Luke's life. Tim Lott has been my dentist for over twenty years and he has been brilliant with Luke, patiently showing him how the dentist chair works and encouraging him to go in separately from me so that he has his own relationship with him. One of the first times that Luke went to see him he gulped down the entire contents of the pink mouth-wash. He had been obsessed with trying out the 'pink fizzy drink' and wasted no opportunity in doing so. Fortunately he has fine teeth, not in any way a reflection on the lack of brushing they get, and has not needed any treatment but familiarity is the key and he has them checked regularly. I asked Luke today when he last brushed his teeth and he had a think, then answered me very sincerely "at least three days ago." I remind him twice a day and try and make sure he does them but as he is now a teenager it is becoming more difficult to manage his personal hygiene, although I still brush his hair, he wouldn't remember otherwise and only this morning I made him use shampoo in the shower. You can get little 'finger puppet' toothbrushes that rub your teeth clean which we recently discovered when we went to a special school for Aspergers Syndrome and the children were being given a personal hygiene lesson.

Dr Murray is the Consultant Community Paediatrician who diagnosed Luke and who we liaise with. We see him every three months, during which he reviews Luke's weight, height and behaviour. He has a gentle and amused manner that calms and reassures me. He is unfazed by Luke's behaviour and that is reassuring in itself. He is available to us on the end of a telephone and will liaise with other health departments, directly if appropriate, although there are always waiting lists to contend with. He prescribes medication for Luke or refers him to Dr Chris Bools, the Consultant in Child and Adolescent psychiatry when anxiety becomes more of an issue. Luke doesn't want to see him at the moment, he is very aware that Dr Murray knows his worst kept secrets and that is awful for a teenager. There is no dignity in autism. His habits, behaviour and life generally are, of necessity, picked over by the professionals who are trying to help him and he finds the facts of that intolerable, as any teenager would.

Dr Chris Bools has treated Luke during his times of acute anxiety. Sometimes these are triggered by specific events and sometimes he just feels generally anxious and unable to cope with day-to-day life. Luke actually has *chronic anxiety* tagged on as an extra label. It debilitates him, making him a very difficult boy to communicate with, to live with. Dr. Bools doesn't have a magic wand but he does seem to reach something in Luke. Again, he has a very gentle, calm, soft approach to Luke and doesn't over-react to things that Luke may or may not say. Luke can say very socially inappropriate things at times and one that springs to mind occurred when we were seeing Dr. Bools just before Christmas. Luke had been unable to attend school due to his acute anxiety, even to the point of vomiting with the strength of his panic attacks. We were both stressed out from lack of sleep and the state of Luke's mind and he was very autistic, turning his back on Dr. Bools and ignoring him completely. I was so miserable and my tears were very close to the surface. It really hurts to see your child like that. Every parent wants their child to be happy and when you can't give your child any kind of happiness or even comfort or cuddle them it is almost unbearable, no matter that it is a fact of life for us. Add to that the other fact of life that they appear to hate you and want to hurt you. I was desperate to help him, reach him. Dr. Bools was making notes on Luke's behaviour when Luke, without appearing to be looking at me, said, "Dr. Bools, my mum is thinking something about you". I blushed because I was, more as a distraction than a direct observation, noticing that he was wearing sandals, which struck me as odd, given the time of year. "Yes" Luke went on "she's thinking that she would like to have sex with you right now." I actually felt relief that Luke had got it wrong, rather than embarrassment at what he had said. Dr. Bools, of course, didn't bat an eyelid, just kept writing. Right response!

Because Dr. Bools is now familiar to Luke, I can leave the room and Luke will talk to him and share his anxieties if he knows what they are. That is a big trust. Dr Bools treats Luke with respect and he appreciates that. Having said that he finds it very hard to talk about home if he is out of the home. Similarly, he can't talk about school at home or vice versa. Ideally he needs home/school visits so that he can deal with his anxieties in the place where they occur at the time that they occur!

The professional who has supported me most in many ways is my hairdresser, Kelly Dillon. She has been in charge of my hair for seven years now and has seen me through the transition from brunette to blond. Being blond is so much easier, no one expects much of me, my memory lapses are firmly put down to blond moments and that suits me just fine. Kelly is wise beyond her years, coming as she does from a family of eight children and there isn't much she doesn't know about anything really. Having said that, she is one of the few people I know who has used her second hand experience to avoid most of life's pitfalls, so far anyway! She is a welcome listening ear and she comes out with gems of information that I wouldn't have known otherwise, plus she makes me look good and that alone makes me feel better.

Interestingly, all the people that Luke relates to best are men! He is just more comfortable with men and regards women as less important. In his black and white view of the world he sees men as the important people who make the money and so hold the power. He has never seen me work and so that is his blueprint for life. The fact that I haven't worked because I have been looking after him is an irrelevance to Luke, it isn't his reality.

Jan's tip: The professionals who deal with our children are very important to us. They can make all the difference, more than they realise probably. (Abbi told me the other day that there is a bus driver called Dan who is always happy and consequently he delivers a busload of happy children to school. I wondered if he realizes his power for good?)

Sameness is so important to autistic children. They like routine, structure and the same face and voice. They are often very sensitive to touch and although they are autistic, they have the same right to respect, even if their behaviour is unusual. We were having some family therapy sessions with a child psychologist and initially Luke's behaviour towards her was atrocious, to the point of crawling through her legs. However he was testing her to see if he could trust her response to him. He was just beginning to get used to her when she left. Since then there hasn't been anyone who has stayed long enough to win his trust and we have been denied that source of help.

The professionals who deal with our children do not have a user-friendly environment. We talk about our children in front of them, describing their worst behaviour and private habits whilst they are expected to sit there quietly! Luke never sits anywhere quietly but least of all under those circumstances.

The National Health Service really needs a huge shake-up in relation to our children. The waiting lists are horrendous, the facilities are basic and the specialists are under-funded and unsupported in their positions. They have no access to specialist teams for autism and yet the rate of diagnosis is at epidemic proportions. Central Government needs to start funding help at ground level from diagnosis onwards. The Government's own document on Autism, issued by the Department of Education and Skills to the Department of Health comes in two parts. It is a very comprehensive document, a good practice guide and says 'Autistic Spectrum disorders are complex and will undoubtedly require the input of different agencies. There should be a multi-agency co-operation and intervention which recognizes the multiple demands ASDs place on providers. Interagency discussion is crucial. For children and their families to receive a coordinated flexible and seamless service, statutory, voluntary and independent providers need to link and liaise across organisational boundaries.' In our experience those are fine words but the reality is anything but.

If you are struggling with your child go to your MP. Go to the top wherever you can. The professionals are doing their job to the best of their limited resources and they are already overworked. Your MP is the person who is elected to make a difference on your behalf. Your local paper should tell you when their surgery is in your area and you can go along and request their help. Alternatively, ask your GP to write letters on your behalf. Ideally, join together with other parents in your area and use people power. If you want a copy of the document mentioned it can be obtained from DfES Publications, PO Box 5050, Sherwood Park, Annesley, Nottingham NG15 0DJ or Email: dfes@prolog.uk.com quoting ref. DfES/597/2002/REV.

It is a sad fact that the health service fails children like Luke and the only way to change the system is to make the people in power aware of our plight. We need professionals who are aware of all the implications of Luke's disability and we need them now, not in two years time.

Lukes tip: I like important people and James Gray is someone who I like because he treats me with respect. I like uniforms because they make me feel safe and you know who someone is then. I don't like people talking about me in front of me. Dr Bools has really helped me to realise that talking is good even though usually when I see him, my first problem is over and I am getting a new one. I always seem to have a problem with my friends or my family or myself and my behaviour.

If I feel very anxious and angry and I don't know why then I find someone to blame because then I can focus my anger on that. Quite often that is my mum. I admit that I am so contrary and sometimes she can never get it right. For example: she tells me why I have upset my friends and I argue with her that she is thick and she doesn't know or understand anything about me and my behaviour. Then she doesn't tell me why I have upset my friends and I shout at her that she is a thick b**** because she never helps me and doesn't explain things to me. I don't know if I can explain this to you but when you are a teenager your mum shouldn't be the person who teaches you. She should just be your mum.

I have definite ideas about most things but I think that I am getting better at understanding that other people don't and I am learning to laugh at myself. That is the answer. I laugh at myself before someone else does and then it is ok and I have control.

Talking of laughing, blond jokes are among my favourites. Did you hear the one about the blond who was so stupid she tried to drown a fish? I have gotten into a heap of trouble with my cousin Heidi, who is a natural blond, for my blond jokes. Some of them are too rude to print.

APPENDIX TO CHAPTER 12   LETTER FROM LUKES GP

To whom it may concern:

Luke Dicker

Dob 6.12.91

Diagnosis: Aspergers Syndrome/ADHD/Chronic anxiety

This young man is registered as my patient and I can confirm that he has the diagnosis listed above. As a result of his illness Luke's behaviour can be quite strange or impulsive and perhaps fall outside what we would normally call socially acceptable!

Luke is a delightful young man, but can be very hard work. Luke and his family are not to blame for his condition so I would respectfully ask that you give them every assistance that you can. Remember Luke will be with you for only a few minutes, his family live with him 24 hours a day.

Luke does not cope well with new situations and finds it very hard to stand in a queue or be in a crowded place surrounded by people he doesn't know for any length of time. These situations will lead to anxiety and Luke will eventually vomit from anxiety unless he can find a place where he can get away and be quiet. I am grateful for any and all help that you can give to Luke and his family.

Yours sincerely

Dr. John Harrison

➤ We have been told that places like Legoland, Disneyland and other theme parks are aware of Aspergers Syndrome and treat it as they would any other disability. So it is worth telling them and getting fast-tracked, which friends of ours have successfully done. For families like ours it makes all the difference.

➤ We have used this letter at airports where Luke is over stimulated and easily agitated. It has been invaluable in those circumstances where we are already stressed and Luke can flip altogether if he isn't removed from the source of his anxiety.

CHAPTER 13 SAD, MAD BUT NOT BAD

This is the defining chapter that says why my boy is so hard to live with. I found it the saddest to write because every mum longs for her child to be happy, healthy and well fed. Above that, you dream of what their life might be when they grow up but so long as you know they are all of the above, that is a mum's heart for their child.

Well, Luke is none of those and I don't dream of his future because we get through each day. That is enough.

Ever since he was a baby and started on solids, Luke would choke on anything that had the tiniest lump in it. He hated most tastes and wanted milk and sucking. That was his ritual, his comfort and he wasn't interested in chewing. (I don't think he has ever learnt to chew properly, in fact.) Then he only wanted one familiar taste. He would spit out most foods so you reverted to the one thing you knew he would take. He has always been like that. Try something new and he spits or vomits it back. Even now if he eats a meal at a restaurant and it has been cooked in the ' wrong oil' or with butter of any sort, he will puke it up. He had a daily bottle of milk long, long, long after he was a baby. It was the only thing that comforted him, settled him and sometimes the only thing he would take. At some level I knew that he needed that degree of comfort and sameness. I so wish someone had reassured me back then and saved me the constant worry of making comparisons. I can't say this enough: instinct is God-given and so undervalued in our society but it is the voice you should listen to as a mum, particularly a new mum and I am so glad that I have acted on my instincts against medical, all other advice because I have been proved right. I don't say that in a 'look at me' sense, just that I was desperate for some reassurance at the time and didn't know if I *was* doing the right thing. Even if your child is normal their development is unique and your instinct is good. Trust it.

Luke's brain takes on blueprints. The first time he tastes something, that is the blueprint. His brain demands that any future taste has to be exactly the same. Same brand, same cooking method, same cooking oil, same, same, same. He eats different foods now because his friends do and yet his brain tells his stomach to reject it and it does. Being sick is as normal to Luke as eating. He is sick when he travels, sick when he eats, sick if something smells too strongly for his over-sensitive nose and sick through nerves. He goes to the bathroom, throws up and then carries on. He does it like he does everything, very loudly, but as it is a normal bodily function to him he treats it as such. I know when he is going to be sick because his face stops dead, goes a whiter shade of the pale it always is and he starts swallowing hard. We always have to know where the nearest toilet is. We always take a carrier bag (hopefully with no holes in the bottom!) with us. He visited my brother Tim in hospital the other day with me, (under duress I might add, he doesn't like hospitals.) As soon as we sat down I knew he would throw up by the look on his face and we had already sussed out where the toilet was. It was the smell. Actually the smell of hospitals makes me feel sick but I can put mind over matter, Luke can't.

He has had a list of safe foods that he will eat and they have been so limited that he would rather starve than eat anything unfamiliar. We have been on holiday and he has eaten nothing and I mean nothing, for days. When your child eats nothing then *anything* becomes ok. Believe me.

Luke's comfort ritual for a long time was a cup of tea and a pile of chocolate digestive biscuits. He would sit down with them, in his own little world and dunk and lick the chocolate off them in a particular way, three at a time. It was partly ritualistic and partly the taste and partly the comfort of sameness and control. We have travelled miles in search of chocolate digestive biscuits in different countries, just to get him to eat. Trouble is they had to be *Mcvities*. He would starve, literally, rather than eat an unfamiliar taste, even a chocolate biscuit. You can take a horse to water but you can't make it drink. The same is true of Luke's relationship with food. His brain dictates to his body what it is allowed to eat. He is trying so hard now to change his blueprints. For the very first time recently he had gravy on a meal. Before then, he would only be able to eat each taste separately and each food had to be plain and not touching the other one. A typical meal would be a piece of broccoli, still the only vegetable he will eat, a piece of meat with absolutely no fat on it and boiled potato. Each food had to be eaten separately and not be touching the next food.

His favourite foods have been eggs, pancakes, tomato ketchup (addicted to the point of climbing onto the kitchen cupboard and licking the top of the bottle), pizza, white bread with no butter ever, *Mcvities* chocolate digestive biscuits and baked beans. O yes and orange juice to drink. He has been addicted to the foods that made his eczema worse and his behaviour worse again.

On a humorous note, he went to tea with James 'bigfoot', (he's the same age as Luke and takes size 13 shoes!) and James' mum Denise phoned me later in bewilderment. She had asked Luke what he would like to eat and he had said pepperoni pizza, which she very kindly provided. Luke had proceeded to pick off all the pepperoni and eat the pizza base and she naturally wondered why. When I asked him later why he had done this he explained that he didn't like pepperoni! He hadn't realised that you could ask for a Margerita pizza with just cheese and tomato and no pepperoni. He thought all pizza was pepperoni because that was the first pizza he had tasted. His logic is his logic.

Luke does not recognise hunger and consequently, (something Luke also does not recognise) he won't eat. "I am not hungry," he would say "but I do have a tummy ache. Can I have some medicine for my tummy ache?" I ask him now where the pain is and when he points to his 'high up tummy' you know he is probably hungry. Persuading him to eat though is a different matter. When he is anxious his taste goes wrong and he can't keep anything down. He also gets very angry when he is hungry so the anxiety attached to feeding him is huge.

If the smell of a food is wrong it won't get past his bloodhound nose, his sense of smell is so acute. He can smell if a food is a different brand and will only eat the familiar one. He will eat toast with honey on it at my mum's, but at home he can't eat that. It is a 'granny' food, not a home food. He says the toast at home doesn't smell the same! He will agree with you that there is no logic. He is as baffled and frustrated by this as anyone else yet all the intelligent reasoning in the world can't overturn his implacable mindset.

The choking and spitting out that accompany a meal is a reflex action for Luke over which he appears to have no control. However, he will now apologise and remove his plate to the kitchen. Small children are brilliant at reacting with complete disgust and very exaggerated behaviour speaks to Luke. What has happened though is that Luke's inbuilt resistance to change and the embarrassment of his eating habits means that you tend to choose the safe option and reinforce his safety in sameness.

There is no comfort zone in feeding him, no pleasures given or received. Just a battleground and I pick the battles more warily now. For Luke, every day eating is an irrelevance which stops him doing what he is doing. It is a social nightmare for him too. If he decides not to eat at all, which he could do, deriving little, if no pleasure from most eating experiences apart from his ritualistic ones, then we have lost the war. He finds the social implications of eating a meal almost impossible at the moment. He has discarded all the routine that we have built up over the younger years and takes his plate off to the safety of his bedroom. It is the biggest sadness for me and yet I have to accept it. Trying to fight it just uses more emotional energy and makes it more, not less of a problem.

The other day I thought we had a victory. He asked for an apple, which he can only eat peeled. The first apple he ever tasted was a Granny Smith and so that is the only apple he will eat. We only had 'red' apples left in the fruit bowl so I peeled one very carefully and cut it into segments and popped it in a bowl for him. He didn't shout his indignation so I thought that he had eaten it and was <u>sooo</u> pleased. Later on that day though, I found the bowl, contents intact, in his clothes cupboard. He told me that the apple had smelt wrong as it wasn't a Granny Smith. However, he hadn't wanted to insult me by rejecting it so had hidden it instead. Actually that in itself was amazing, that he had thought of my feelings. Progress of a sort! But a parenting dilemma. Did I tell him off for hiding it or praise him for thinking of my feelings? Nothing with him is straightforward.

We have seen a dietician and also Dr Murray monitors Luke's weight and height at three monthly intervals (if Luke can bring himself to come to the clinic) and he is relatively healthy but his diet is dire.

Luke loves chocolate but it has to be *Cadburys* dairy milk and he will only eat it melted. It is such a restrictive part of his and our life, this mindset that dictates just exactly what he can or can't eat and how and when and where. It has dominated every holiday, every other day too. I will cook a meal tonight and Luke will look at it and he may or may not eat it. Even if he is starving hungry, he doesn't recognize hunger. He may not like the look of the food because it should look the same, smell the same, taste the same as always. My lovely friend Aura asked him once if he liked sausages and he said yes. She cooked some sausages but they weren't the same as the ones I cook so he couldn't eat them, even though he knew that it was 'insulting to her cooking' as he put it. How do you explain it to people?

They don't understand and it is interesting to see how personally some people take it when he rejects their food. If people make an issue of it with him now he is older, that just increases his dislike of the social aspects of eating and makes him even more reluctant to try something different.

As a mum, I don't know if I can convey to you the sheer frustration of preparing food for him only to have it spat out or rejected. The upset of never having happy family mealtimes. The ridiculousness of seeing him eat his paper serviette in preference to his meal. And then there's the awful reality of his daily diet and the worry of it too. You get to the point where you just have to switch off or go crazy. At times it makes me feel numb and hard, because it is such an unnatural thing for a mum to do. I still get just as mad though when my food is rejected. Like I say, understanding Luke doesn't make him any easier to live with!

He decided to make some cakes the other day. They were the packet type, the ones that are easy to make for someone with the attention span of a flea. Abbi had been very sick for three days with a tummy bug. I had used the cake-making bowl as her sick bowl because since we left **'The Edge'** our kitchen cupboard space has halved and we only have one bowl. She had been so very sick that the last time had been just spit and bile (excuse the detail!). I went to the kitchen to switch the oven on, still carrying the bowl, contents intact, on my way to empty and disinfect it when the phone rang. It was my friend Wendy, a very welcome distraction. We chatted and laughed and when I came off the phone Luke proudly informed me that his cakes were in the oven. That was a big achievement for him, a first I think. When we took them out of the oven I suddenly had the awful thought of "Luke, did you use the cake bowl?" to which he replied the inevitable "Yes". "Did you wash it out first?" I asked, already knowing the answer. Negative. He has never washed up anything in his life willingly, himself included. We threw the cakes away, to the accompanying tantrum from Luke, needless to say, and he spent the rest of the evening throwing up, he had licked the bowl out with no problem - sick being a familiar taste to him! Disgusting but true and you have to laugh, what else can you do?

Luke's temper is scary, both to him and us. His tantrums have been a fact of our family life and he can be very violent towards both Abbi, myself and ours/his possessions. He has smashed anything and everything, mostly in frustration, including his head against the floor. When he got his last prescription pair of glasses at Boots opticians I was offered insurance at

£18 a year to replace broken pairs. That was a wonderful piece of news for me and I availed myself of the offer immediately. The only proviso was that I had to hand in the old glasses when claiming a new pair and so I have, several times. The problem is that by the time Luke has finished with them they bear absolutely no resemblance to a pair of glasses whatsoever and the nice lady who seems to serve me every time tries to look as though it is perfectly normal to receive a mangled mash of metal with no glass in sight. My skin is growing thicker by the visit.

We have had holes kicked in the walls, doors completely trashed, plants snapped in half, holes cut in the sofa and the cushions, his metal bed frame is seriously dented, the list goes on. When we first moved into this little house with its' cream! carpets, Luke emptied a jar of maple syrup on the lounge carpet (whilst I was taking Abbi to school) in protest at being left alone. It is when he uses something as a weapon that I get really frightened. Dr Bools has prescribed Respiradol so that I can medicate him and knock him out if his violence is life threatening.

I phoned the local police when he held a big kitchen knife to me on a very, very bad day when he couldn't go to school and was prowling around the house in a state of high anxiety. They were lovely, very understanding and having disarmed Luke and talked to him calmly and kindly, they came back to return the knife the next day and to check that we were all right. Social Services were informed of the incident at my request and at long last, I thought we might get the help I had been asking them for but I'm glad I didn't hold my breath. We had a couple of home assessment visits where the size of our house and the origins of our nationality seemed more relevant than the scale of our problems, then waited for a long period of time to receive a report by post that made all sorts of recommendations, including what social clubs there are for teenagers in Malmesbury! I wondered if they had any grasp whatsoever of our situation and that's the last we've heard, even though Abbi is both a young carer and a child at risk of Luke's temper. The only person I know who gets respite care for her hyperactive stepson dumped him on Social Services doorstep and told them to look after him. Who wants to resort to such desperate measures when you spend your life trying to cope in the extreme and protect your child's dignity into the bargain? Our children are the vulnerable members of society through no fault of their own and the violence is an expression of frustration. A society that abandons its' elderly and its' vulnerable is no society at all.

Luke is not a bad boy. He isn't naughty although his behaviour is awful, but that is his disability and underneath he is actually a very polite and charming individual who has strong morals and deep feelings. Hopefully as he gets older, that side of him will become more apparent.

Jan's tip: food remains a difficult and emotional subject and I have had to learn how to detach myself, against all my maternal instincts, from worrying about it because making it an issue gives Luke additional anxiety and that exacerbates any problem. He appears to be *relatively* healthy although he has constant catarrh and is always very pale and usually constipated too, but those symptoms seem to go hand in hand with Aspergers Syndrome anyway. I think his constitution is different to ours and it would appear that his body can survive on next to nothing at all. He has always been excessively thirsty and does drink a lot of water. Drinking has always been more important to him than eating.

I have been told by the police and various other people involved with the community that the only way to get help is to shout long and loud, to make a nuisance of yourself! That is easier for some people than others. Actually, I've been told that you'd be better off if you didn't speak English in your own country because then someone would come and offer you all the help you need, especially with dreaded form-filling, so maybe that is the best tip of all. Pretend to be either illiterate or a refugee. Discrimination in Blair's Britain is a two-way street. Cool Britannia.

Luke's tip: Cool is a teenage word. Anyone over the age of about nineteen who uses that word is sad.

I will find it very hard to talk about my anger because it is a horrible part of me and yet I want to try and explain it. I don't know how to control my feelings because they are so strong and whatever is happening to me is the only thing I know about. If I want to do something I want to do it *now* and I don't know any way of waiting calmly. You can talk to me about it and I will agree with you about counting to ten and all those kind of things but when my feelings are that strong I just can't control my response and that may be the next minute. My anger boils up and out of me and I can feel the muscles in my arms going tight and my hands curl into fists. I have had boxing gloves and all sorts of things to try and take my anger out on and they have been helpful, sometimes. It all depends on where I am and who has made me angry. When I was little the best thing was to take me away from the circumstance and lock me in my room until I had calmed down, even though it was horrible at the time but it worked because it stopped me from doing anything worse to someone. At the moment at home I take a hammer and smash it into the grass or the mud and that helps me to get my anger out. I have been very frightened that I would kill someone in my temper and I used to dream that I had and wake up with my heart thumping. I think I am getting better at controlling my temper but it still takes me over and I would love to take it over. My aim is to be liked at least and loved at best.

Abbi's tip: me and mum have been hurt by Luke lots of times and sometimes living with him has been like I imagine hell to be. The worst part is that we have been very frightened of him, but when he calms down he is fine and wants to make up straight away. We are still in shock though, especially if he has been very violent and smashed things and hurt us and it takes us a lot longer to forget it than Luke.

CHAPTER 14 CALL ME NIGEL

Obsessions are a recognised trait of Aspergers Syndrome and fortunately, as Luke has grown, his obsessions have grown with him (apart from the one constant - his all-time hero, more of which later). That is better, I think, than being bored rigid with the same one if you don't share it, which, chances are, you won't! He has two forms of obsessions: - a current interest about which he will talk incessantly if allowed, and his obsessive ritualistic behaviour or habits. He is totally obsessed with whatever the current thing is, but at least with him it changes with the mood. It started (predictably enough) with *Thomas the Tank Engine*, progressing at some stage to Dinosaurs-so boring. (Whoever thought up all the different versions of dinosaurs must have a brain the size of a brachiosaurus, the size of a walnut. Yeah right, the theory of a brain that size to control a creature the size of four London buses that poos enough to cover a city the size of London every week all on a diet of plants beggars belief! Only a boy would be obsessed with such stuff.) We have lived with too many interests to list here but all of them have been equally important to Luke and all of them much more real to him than the world that the rest of us inhabit. He becomes obsessed to the point that it is all he thinks about and he has to try and make it as literal as possible.

A lasting obsession though is money. Luke realised very early on in life its' importance in our materialistic society and its' value as a negotiating tool. (Remember Luke's logic is caveman style.) Because he is so smart he negotiates everything, even his behaviour and he always asks for more because that is his literality, negotiate to win. It can make asking him to do even the simplest thing very complicated when everything has to be bartered over - the most mundane of tasks has a price tag to Luke.

His school had a tabletop sale in the local town hall and Luke rented himself a table top for £5, set himself up in his best *'Del Boy'* impersonation and made more money than anyone else there. I think he came home with over £60 and that was after reserving goods at another stall until he had made the money to pay for them out of his earnings. He even went out into the street and persuaded people to come in and buy, (bribing them with the offer of some free wax crayons which he had been given a job lot of) and he worked really hard because his motivation was top notch. Money in his pocket. However, one person who he couldn't persuade to purchase anything was James Gray, our MP (he's Scottish by birth!) who was holding a surgery in another part of the building. That didn't faze Luke though, who got his monies worth in a different way by jumping the queue - you remember he doesn't queue - and going in for a consultation instead, telling James that his parents' marriage was falling apart and asking for his help to fix it! as I later found out, much to my embarrassment.

'*Only Fools and Horses*' has been a lasting obsessive interest and Luke went through a phase of wearing gold rings all the time on every finger, purchased very cheaply from Argos, until he was banned from wearing them at school, thank goodness! That is why it is so important for Luke to have good male role models because he models himself so literally on his heroes. He even talks like them, accent and all and I was so glad, no offence to lovely jubbly David Jason, (whose autograph he has on his bedroom wall courtesy of Tristan Cork) when that one was past its' sell by.

My friend Cathy has just written a song entitled 'Looking for Heroes' which says in a beautifully poetic that we all need heroes, and I suspect boys need them more than girls. Luke is so vulnerable to any kind of strong message though and the wrong idol could easily ruin him.

Jeremy Clarkson is a big hero to Luke, both literally and figuratively. He is larger than life, politically incorrect in a refreshingly funny and very male way and Luke shares his sense of humour, loves his irreverence, his love of cars and caustic comments. Humour is a big tool in getting Luke to laugh at himself and his idiosyncratic ways and in not taking himself too seriously, which he is prone to do, especially when anxious, as we all are. As Luke lives life to the extreme, his emotions live there too.

My guess is that he will find a way to make money for himself. He has that kind of focus and his motivation to succeed is huge. However, it all depends on his self-esteem which can be knocked badly when he is misunderstood. That is why an education will secure him credibility and the right kind of education for a boy like Luke is a life education, not just an academic one. He can be the smartest person with the best ideas but unless he possesses the necessary social skills, it will be much harder, maybe almost impossible, for him to succeed in the cut-throat world of business.

Luke's obsessions completely take him over and they are impossible to fight. He is obsessed with *Star Wars* at the moment and we have been here before. He walks, talks like the character he is most enamoured with, eats like them and has to dress as close to the real thing as possible. He has to possess the necessary figures and re-enact the scenes in his head and he will set himself up with his props anywhere that is the most realistic terrain to satisfy his mental blueprint, even on the stairs. Woe betides anyone who touches him or his figures and disrupts his mindset.

Last Sunday we came out of church and all the boys went to play football outside. Luke cut an odd figure on the pitch with a light sabre in each hand. He wanted to join in but in his own inimitable autistic way! The other boys, bless them, accepted his presence and took it in their stride. Christians should be much more inclined to accept Luke and if they don't, one has to ask why bear the name? Jesus Christ was the ultimate champion of the underdog, going out of his way to find them, validate them and give them acceptance. He was no behaviour snob and the whole of the calendar of our civilisation is based around his life. The Gospels hold beautiful accounts of his care and compassion.

I have always had to fight to pull my boy back to 'normal'. It has been a constant daily, sometimes minute-by-minute battle and on his 'bad' days it has taken all my available energy and some. I know the days, however, when I am wasting my time, even now and then I just have to leave him to his world of make-believe. Until he became a teenager he wouldn't recognize any signals that his body was telling him so he would wet himself and would be unable to eat anything, so absorbed was he in his own little world. Nowadays, he is more easily distractible as he employs the intelligent part of his brain to break into that world. He can still get really mad though, if we break in when he is totally absorbed. His brain has no natural flexibility of its own. "You f***ing bitch" he will shout "I will f***ing kill you" and Abbi and I know that he will try to, until his anger has receded. Then he will be sorry, always and explain how it feels to him when the world in his head is invaded by reality. It hurts his brain like a physical hurt and the shock to his nervous system is as big. His body is beginning to understand itself now and his brain is beginning to recognise the signals that tell him when he is tired, hungry, thirsty, upset, etc. It has taken this long and it is so rewarding to watch him think for himself, at least sometimes.

He still has a bedroom full of figures and cars and enters his little fantasy world with ease (once he has located the necessary figure amongst the chaos). It is quite interesting to see the disparity between the toddler that he often still is emotionally and the teenager that his body is becoming displayed quite clearly in the debris on his bedroom floor.

When Luke's mind is really agitated he lines his cars or figures up and that is his way of controlling his world. He reduces it down to a row of cars which are perfectly lined up on the bathroom floor and he will get out of the shower and lie on the floor, soaking wet and yet oblivious to anything/everything whilst he creates his own order out of the confusion that inhabits his brain. This is so frustrating when he is meant to be getting ready, usually for school and instead he is locked in the bathroom, living in the world inside his head. Sometimes there is no reaching him and those days disturb me because he is unrecognisable as the boy that you see. He is another boy, a very autistic boy who is locked in his own world. There is no way of communicating to him the tenderness those days evoke in me however, as he is totally unaware of human contact. He explains to me that he still needs those days to regain his equilibrium, to retreat into his own safety and then he comes back to our world when he is ready. Those days are fewer and farther between at the moment but we go in cycles and just when you think that things are improving, we beat the retreat.

I can't tell you how much I love him and what an emotional roller coaster we ride together. Yet the autism keeps us apart, denying him physical contact, eye contact, and me the chance to hold him, cuddle him, kiss it all better. It feels like I'm betraying him when I tell someone else how he is in his most private moments, although my motive for doing so is only for his good. If we have a rare appointment to see someone on a good day, then that professional would think that Luke has hardly any disability. He can be bright, articulate and informative, if a little inappropriately at times. In any case, no one sees him on his really bad days because he can't leave the house, or even his bedroom. In the really bad times it is hard to believe that things will get better. Particularly when he is violent towards us and lately, himself. He talks about killing himself, about his lack of self-worth and how everything he does is misunderstood or backfires on him. As he lives life to the extreme, there is no middle ground. He is either depressed or highly excitable but rarely anything in between. As I write though, he is on the third consecutive day of being happy and coping with life and since becoming a teenager, that is a first, so there is always hope!

When he was younger he would be a different character every day and would face the world as *Super Ted* or *Superman* or whichever character he decided to be. This was his safety. He didn't know who Luke was so he became a character that he had watched very carefully on TV, so he knew exactly how to behave. He said to me once "Mummy I don't know who I am, I can't see myself". So he would have to dress like a character that he could see, to literally become them in his mind and he still does this, even now. He went through a stage of being obsessed with *WWF* wrestling and would have to dress in character for each bout of wrestling with the life-size dummy that I made for him. Sometimes, he would have twelve bouts in as many minutes and the debris of each costume change would be littering the house. He will use anything and everything to be as literal as possible in his dressing up and has often cut things up for the purpose. You never walk into a room after Luke and find it intact. He can't leave cushions on chairs. That is an obsession that drives me mad. He can't be in a room without putting the lights on and having the door shut but he never shuts the door when he leaves a room. He even walks out of the house and leaves the front door wide open as he did this morning!

Luke's 'chewing' has been a nightmare. One of his obsessive habits is to chew, masticate and sometimes spit out or sometimes swallow the object, whatever that may be. He chews paper, towels, clothes, bandages, toys, bits of plastic, rubber, Lego pieces - the list is endless. I have picked up more soggy, chewed up bits of everything from everywhere than one person should have to. Yuck. He had to go to the doctors the other day because his diet inevitably means bowel problems, which seem to go hand in hand with his condition anyway. We had the bizarre conversation of what he had actually eaten in the past few days. Three pieces of Lego, part of a sleeve, several pieces of tissue, maybe some plastic from the crate in his bedroom. Food was the last thing on his list of things consumed, and the look on the locum's face was a picture that made me laugh. We are so used to Luke by now that it is only when someone else reacts that we realise just how bizarre some of his habits are.

He eats his school uniform sleeves and I mean eats them, up to the elbow. The shop that supplies his uniform loves him! They asked me to get the sweatshirts put on the school lunch menu, so good for business! This chewing has been one of Luke's ways of keeping in perpetual motion whilst sitting still and represents just some of the effort that he has to put into managing himself at school. One night I went to bed and just burst into tears. The last straw after a day when Luke hadn't eaten any food at all was to discover that he had climbed into my bed and chewed the top off my bedspread, which I really loved, before falling asleep in my bed. To wake him would be to have yet another sleepless night so, to add insult to injury, I then had to leave him sleeping peacefully in my cosy but chewed-up bed whilst I went to try and sleep in his bunk bed. It would have been easier to accept if he were a dog! That's the frustration of life with Luke. You understand why he has done something but still have to live with the effects. It is a constant balancing act, trying to teach him to face the consequences of his behaviour without giving him a hang-up over it when most of it is unintentional or habitual or through total frustration. There is also the constant worry that something he eats will block his bowel up and whenever he gets a bad tummy ache I am prepared for the worst. So far, so good though!

Snorting is another habit that drives me to despair but the more you mention it, the more Luke snorts, loudly! So I have to try and ignore it but then other people react with disgust and that makes me sad because if he could stop, he would and if I could stop him I would, believe me. We talked about it this morning and he said that it annoys him as much as it does me. He asked me whether he should try and go back to rolling his eyes to the side, to see if that would replace the compulsion to snort! What a choice, eye rolling or snorting! It is funny, in an absurd kind of way. Spitting used to be a problem and he was nearly excluded from school for it until Julie Dyer, the head teacher of a special school in Chippenham helped us. She told me to teach him to spit into his hand if he felt the compulsion to spit at school and that actually enabled him to stop for two reasons. Firstly, because he felt in control of his compulsion and secondly, because he was the one left with a handful of nasty spit! These are the kind of things that we need specialist help for.

One of Luke's most annoying habits involves sellotape, or any kind of sticky tape and string, wool or something to tie or stick things up with. If all else fails he uses my dental floss even though he knows it will send me sky high with rage when I find an empty reel at bedtime. He has always had the compulsion to stick things together or tie things up and to him, it is the most obvious and logical habit in the world. He doesn't see why we all don't do it. I've lost count of the number of times I have broken my nails picking pieces of sellotape off door knobs, window panes and just about everything else around the house. He sticks things together, even the cutlery and the sound of a reel of sellotape being unwound in our house is like the screech of nails down a blackboard, although that comment ages me! White boards don't have the same effect. Just lately he has had an obsession with nail clippers and has cut holes in his pyjamas, his sheets, the cushions and even the leather sofa whilst 'fiddling' with them.

It is the little things that drive you crazy about Luke. The many big dramas, the hyperactivity, the impulsiveness, the constant noise, the mess, all of those we have had to learn to live with and accommodate, just about. BUT when I want to use my nail clippers, my stapler, tweezers, any of those useful things that I keep at the ready and I find them missing or another empty reel where the sellotape should be, well that is the thing that tips the scales. It's the same for Abbi. She copes with so much and takes it in her stride but if he has been into her bedroom and taken her sellotape, well that does it for her too. I have tried buying Luke his own reel of sellotape but this just fuels his obsession and he feels compelled to empty that roll as soon as it is stickingly possible to do so.

Luke has ritualistic behaviour habits too, which could have controlled us as a family if we had let them but we have never been organised and, looking back, I really think that this has helped him to be more adaptable. He has craved routine to the point of sameness and we have had many more fights as a result but his brain is so inflexible that I think he would have narrowed us and himself down to a very few options if we had gone down that route. My personality just cannot provide that level of sameness, I don't do dull and I need the stimulation of change, of being impulsive and finding fun in the moment. It is so important to find a balance because Luke's needs are very dominant. Paul used to say that Luke was the tail that wagged the dog and so the dog has to bark back and sometimes even bite. It's called survival.

His hero of all time is **Nigel Mansell**. Luke knows more about him than Nigel remembers about himself, I bet. As a little boy he insisted on being called Nigel and he wouldn't answer to anything else! He is a walking fount of knowledge on F1 racing in general and his technical know-how is amazing. The first time he drew a racing car, as a little boy, he drew a perfectly symmetrical, bird's eye view of a car, his own perspective! This is a lasting obsession and one that he can turn to at any time but as he has matured he realises that not everyone shares his interest in Mansell. As Luke is offended by anyone who doesn't agree with his intransient point of view, he now protects his own feelings by not talking about Mansell, unless he finds a fellow admirer and he can sniff them out. His form tutor said that Mansell was big, which he was for a racing driver, but Luke thought he meant fat and took that as a personal insult to his choice of hero. He still bears a grudge to this day, a big 'fat' grudge, so be warned Mr. Bradshaw! The day that he met Nigel Mansell, his all-time British hero, at the NEC Birmingham Auto-sport show is the only time in his life that he has been speechless, to date. Luke is unfashionably (thanks to New Labour) deeply patriotic, 'imperialistic' even, according to his latest school report, so to have a hero who is British, is for him, the ultimate in hero worship and he just doesn't understand why everyone doesn't feel that way too.

Every day is a social learning curve for Luke and some days he just can't cope with a world that to him is a puzzle and a battleground. His habits and obsessions seem bizarre to us but to him they are a fact of his life. He says that he has to join our world all the time but who ever joins him in his world? He trusts very few people, a select handful and if you are trusted then you are really honoured because that means you have passed the highest test of all. Luke knows that you love him for himself and he trusts you to take the rough with the smooth, knowing that he wants to please you even if his behaviour says the opposite.

Jan's tip: For us, to fight and challenge Luke's need for ritual and his incessant habits has been the right approach as he enters adolescence. Before this point I wouldn't have known whether what we were doing was being cruel to be kind or not but as he is growing up I can honestly say that from where we are now, it is paying dividends. It has taken an inordinate amount of energy, but it has pulled him back to somewhere approaching normal and if he is ever to gain acceptance in the real world, he needs that balance. Because he is so aware of his differences, we have tried to give him his own perspective on them, enabling him to laugh at himself and to see that, although he is different, he can choose to try and conform when out there in the big world. When he is at home I have tried to give him a safe environment to be himself, to beat the retreat when it all gets too much. This is a difficult place to inhabit though and he still has to respect the rules, (which he insists are stuck up on the kitchen door so he can refer to them) and try and fit in when possible, for our sakes too. He does take some serious living with and sometimes my patience snaps and I shout at him for doing something that I have given him the freedom to do. With his literal interpretation of everything, that confuses him so much that it can send him off on a spiral of very destructive behaviour because he senses the emotion behind my response. This is why it is so vital for us to have specialist help, which we are still asking for.

Luke's tip: I am controlled by my brain and I know now that I get obsessive. When I was younger it was so pointless arguing with me because I had no control over my emotions and if I wanted something I wanted it and I couldn't accept any other truth. So I would throw a tantrum and words were totally wasted. The only way to deal with me was to say NO, mean NO and just lock me in my bedroom to wear myself out because I would attack and fight so hard. Because I don't feel emotion in the same way as you do, that is my kind of logic and it makes sense to me. My mum tried to explain everything to me and I didn't even hear her words, just her voice blah, blah, blahing on and on and it used to make me madder still. My dad used to pick me up, throw me in my room and lock the door. That is the right approach! My mum still doesn't get it, she thinks that everyone 'feels' like her but I don't. Actually what she should have done was to write NO on a piece of paper and shove it in my face. I understand seeing things much better than hearing things. If I see something it is a strong message but words to me mean 'room for an argument'. My mum uses words but I understand black or white and that is my logic.

If I think there is the faintest chance that I can win, I only play to win, so I will try and try and try and try. But if I know that I can't win I will give up now straight away because that is my logic. I am very competitive though and I hate to lose. When I am obsessed with something I honestly can't think about anything else and everything that happens relates back to my interest. But my interests are changing as I grow up. At the moment I am much better at finding age appropriate things to be obsessed with and that means I can fit in better with my friends at school. I am a teenager so I want to act like one.

Abbi's tip: because my brother acts so strangely sometimes and looks so weird when he dresses in different costumes, I only have a few friends that I trust to sleep over. They are my close friends and although, like my mum, I have lots of friends I only invite my trusted ones home. I don't like Luke's behaviour but I am protective of him, he is my brother and he deserves respect. I try and explain him but even grown-ups don't understand so I have to know that my friends can cope with him because he hates people coming into what he thinks of as his territory and he tries to make them scared so they don't come again!!

CHAPTER 15 EDUCATION, WAR AND PEACE

In the past a lot of children with ADHD and probably Aspergers Syndrome too, would have been labelled as awkward, difficult, remedial even. They would have carried that image of themselves into adulthood and would have had no real understanding of their differences and no sympathy for what we now know is a disability. On that basis, our children should have an advantage. We now recognise that behaviour is a child's way of communicating and labels should make it easier for them to succeed, whilst acknowledging their differences.

However, in the lottery that is Central Government funding for Education, our county of Wiltshire is nearly bottom of the table. If your local education authority has a limited budget as ours do, they have many demands on that budget. So they become the 'other side' because they have to decide how best to allocate their limited resources, who gets help and what help is appropriate within the constraints of their budget. They are therefore on the defensive and we, as parents, are made to feel on the offensive, fighting for our children's needs to be met. Apply those economics to the worry of whether your child has a future or not, to having to fight for that future alongside the daily sadness of accepting their condition and it is enough to finish off all but the bravest or the loudest or the richest and that is what they bank on. They have to under the present system. It's a question of economics. Supply and demand. Well, we are supplying an awful lot more of these children on the autistic spectrum for some reason, so let's hope someone in authority wakes up to the demand that will place on the system. We will all be the losers otherwise.

I am passionately convinced that a child who is diagnosed with an autistic spectrum disorder should *automatically* be given a Statement of Special Educational Needs. This Statement could then be tailored to meet that child's need, in conjunction with their particular place on the spectrum. Some children will need no specific help other than just the recognition of their condition, some children require only a safe place to retreat to at break and lunch times. Luke needs much more support, just in organising his possessions for a start, let alone in coping with the change of classrooms, which books to take to each lesson, where and when. Not to mention learning about being sociable, which is a subject in a class of its' own. Or it should be for children like Luke and even more so in mainstream schools.

The last year of Luke's junior school life should have been about identifying what support Luke needed to move on to secondary school and then reassuring him that he would get it, **not** spent as it was, fighting the Local Education Authority in order to prove that his special educational needs actually *existed* in the first place. His primary school head teacher spent a long time helping me with the documentation necessary to try and convince the LEA that Luke needed help and quickly too! We should all have been working together, saving valuable resources, especially human ones, instead of fighting each other. It seems incredible too, that the LEA had to appoint its' own experts to make reports on Luke, going into school and studying him, putting him under even more stress, when he is seen by the NHS experts on a regular basis. Why can't their reports be used when they have in-depth and regular appointments with Luke? It appears to be the case that education and health are at war too, again it's a question of fighting over money, but peace is a lot cheaper all ways round, isn't it?

An interesting point here too, study Luke one day and see an entirely different Luke from the next day. The only predictable thing about him is his unpredictability and just when you expect to see him at his worst, he can produce exemplary behaviour and vice versa. So to commission an expensive and time-consuming report from an Educational Child Psychologist, spending a whole day at school with him, asking him questions to which he will give completely random answers, depending on his mood in that minute, and then assessing his behaviour on the strength of that report is both costly and just so out of context!

Even Dr. Murray, Consultant Paediatrician, who has seen Luke over many years now, is deemed to be on the 'other side' for the LEA's purposes and isn't allowed to make any recommendations re his educational needs! Our GP, Dr. John Harrison, wrote a long letter to the LEA detailing the effects of this time on our family and in particular, the effect it was having on Luke's already fragile state of mind. James Gray, our MP also wrote to the LEA for us. My file of paperwork for just trying to obtain an educational statement of special needs for Luke is four inches thick. Imagine the amount of report writing, letter writing, telephone calls, meetings, specialist reports, the sheer hard graft time factor involved in that file and all for one little boy to gain just the *recognition* of his need for help at school because *his* brain doesn't process information in the same way as the rest of us! Makes you wonder who has the problem!

The whole experience was an awful one, a huge waste of resources and it cost us our family life as Luke fell apart and had the equivalent of a nervous breakdown. Poor little boy.

He just couldn't cope with the idea of change and not knowing who, if anyone, would be helping him adjust to life at such a 'Big' school of 1200 pupils. It was all just too much for him to comprehend. At our village school of 150 pupils he was known by everyone, he had a teaching assistant with him at all times who explained each circumstance to him as it happened so that he could try to make sense of everything and he was *still* struggling to cope. He had stabbed a knife in my hand one day and there were big gouges out of the dining room wall where he had thrown chairs at me in his rage and frustration. We were truly living in a war zone at home and it was thanks, in no small part, to the LEA. They finally issued us with a statement giving him non-specialist help for 25 hours a week, at the end of August, just *two weeks* before he was due to start at senior school. Bearing in mind that I had initiated the application for Luke to be statemented at the beginning of September the *previous* year, their timing seemed downright cruel. Our summer holidays were spent in a state of *extreme* anxiety with Luke's need to know just who was going to be looking after him, how he would relate to them or most importantly, if he could even trust them with himself. What a big worry for any boy, let alone a little boy who hated change at the best of times.

My friend Liz, who lives in our village, has a son who was diagnosed as profoundly deaf at an early age. He has had one to one specialist help by a fully trained professional who speaks his language throughout pre-school and for the duration of his school life. He has displayed frustrated behaviour that everyone understands because his disability is understood. She has had the opposite experience to us with Nathan's education and yet who is the most disabled child? Why should we have to fight the system to try and prove that Luke's disability is as profound as it is because his behaviour *is* his disability?

I can only tell it like it has been for us. I really hope that your Local Education Authority has made better provision for children like Luke than Wiltshire CC. One thing is certain. We live in the wrong place for a child with special needs on the autistic spectrum. The deputy headmistress of Luke's secondary school told me to move county if we wanted any kind of specialist help with Luke's education (and that was after she had excluded him for a day without even realising he had a statement). Wiltshire has no specialist provision in county and consequently, a disproportionate amount of their budget is spent on sending a few children out of county on specialist placements. This means that they stand no chance, without additional Central Government funding, of ever having the resources to fund a specialist autistic centre in county. It also means that the amount of money left over for the majority of pupils has to be fought over, scrapped over, in our experience. What happens to the losers in this, the 21st century?

The irony is that Luke couldn't wait to start primary school, to be a big boy and wear the uniform. He loves uniforms; they speak of position, of authority, of power. They are fact. He loves to pin my grandad's medals from the 2nd world war on his chest. They represent achievement and recognition and pride to Luke. They are measurable. (His communication is mainly visual whereas mine is auditory and so we have been speaking a different language - which I have only just realised as I write!)

He *ran* to our village school in his uniform for the first few days, proud and pleased to be there. However, it didn't take past the first week for him to say "I've done school now Mummy, I don't want to go anymore". It was such an alien environment for him and has been ever since. To sit still, to concentrate, to conform, to try and fit in. None of those things meant anything to him and he knew he was different, even then. He was the first child in his reception class to start writing phonetically but he had no interest in reading whatsoever until the first *Harry Potter* book came out when he was eight and he picked it up and read it straight through in three days! He would come out of school, throw his bag at me and do a runner, full of anger and pent-up energy. One day he came out of school and I was talking to someone, a crime in Luke's book - my attention was for him alone - so he attacked me from behind. Before I knew it I was flat on the floor. He had launched himself at me, grabbed my throat and just pulled me backwards. He was so angry, misunderstood and frustrated and he wanted me to know how he felt, so he made my life a misery because he didn't have the faintest idea how to put those strong feelings into words. He cried every morning, loud and long when I eventually got him to school and he clung to me and had to be prised off. Then when I picked him up again he was spitting mad with me for abandoning him and he was out to make me pay.

There have been very few days since then that Luke has been ok with the idea of school. It has been an emotional nightmare. If your child is unhappy then you are unhappy. I have had to fight him to get his clothes on only for him to pull them all off again, morning after morning. With his literality, if he didn't have his uniform on he couldn't go to school so he would undress as soon as I had dressed him. He would bite me and scratch me and fight me and we would get to school having left one war zone only to enter the emotional one where he would cry and plead and beg me not to leave him.

Every day I felt like a traitor and I still do, all these years later. I had tears in my eyes today just like I have on all the other days that I have had to make Luke go to school. It's a mum thing. Your job as a mum is to protect your child. I can't protect Luke from his worst fear. Not only can't I protect him but I have to make him face his worst fear day in, day out. I see the pale face, the withdrawal of personality, the stomach churning, which means he can't eat any breakfast and the all too familiar signs of aggression that hide his anxiety. Whether his fears have any basis in our reality or not, they are very real to him. He hates the change of environment from home to school. Home is where Luke can be Luke, all the different versions and some. Home is safe and predictable and controllable. School is where Luke has to be the other Luke. Because he is smart, he understands about wanting to conform but the effort it takes him to do that is huge and so, when he gets home, he lets out all the pent up energy and aggression that he has been trying to keep under wraps all day. The next day it starts all over again and it must take so much effort, just to try to fit in.

Standing in the playground at primary school with Luke attached to my leg, trying to look like a regular mum, yet so cut up inside that tears were just a kind word away, my physical exhaustion at this time was total. Gradually, his teachers, who were very experienced, started to adopt methods to deal with him and he was always placed close to the teacher, usually by himself and given extra attention. He really flourished in years three and four when he had male teachers and he responded to their very direct and humorous ways of teaching plus his brain was being challenged. Mr. Philcox was the best teacher for Luke. He was young and handsome and appealed to the children enormously. (The mums liked him too for some reason!) He had a great sense of humour along with a keen grip on discipline, which kept the large number of village boys in Luke's class highly motivated, Luke included.

I am also passionately convinced that for *some* children on the autistic spectrum, the demands of mainstream school are too high. Luke started to fall apart in year five. He just flipped and his anxiety became so bad that he had migraines, panic attacks to the point of vomiting and was such a sad little boy that Dr. Murray referred him to Dr. Chris Bools, Consultant in child psychiatry and *chronic anxiety* became another label to add to his existing two. He had a male teacher in this year also but he couldn't relate to him at all and he was becoming much more aware of the wider world and in particular, the reality of having to change schools at the end of year six. He was so out of control that he was dangerous really, not only to himself but to the other children too. I started to keep him out of school when I knew that he was dangerously close to losing it there, but that meant that I was his victim at home instead, the lesser of two evils. I just couldn't bear the awful reality of him hitting someone we knew at school and the subsequent trauma. In retrospect, I probably should have let that happen, awful as it would have been, because then the LEA would have had to address his level of disability sooner, rather than later. However, it is easy to be wise with the cold blood of hindsight but without the emotions you were experiencing at the time. I wish with all my heart that the system worked for us and not against us when we live with such acute difficulties anyway. The irony of it is that the harder I work to make Luke socially acceptable, the less help we get.

One day at this time, Luke was actually at school and his friends were playing football against a neighbouring school. Luke wanted to play but he couldn't be included in the team for two reasons. One, he simply couldn't be part of a team, he doesn't know how to interact to that degree and two, even if he did he was too emotionally unpredictable. His friend James asked Luke to distract their goalie as a way of making him feel a valid part of the proceedings and the match started. Luke took James literally, how else would he take anything? He asked the goalie what he thought of the war in Iraq, a reasonable distracting tactic to Luke and he explained very politely that he wanted a reasoned answer in return. The other boy, aged ten, told him to "p*** off weirdo", as boys do, at which Luke took great offence. He tore off his school shirt, ripping it from top to bottom and then marched onto the pitch with the intention of killing the goalie and saving the school's honour. One of the other mums rugby tackled Luke off the pitch (I had my shoulder in a sling at the time, having dislocating it skiing) and saved us the awful embarrassment of a school incident. Luke then ran away, as he always did and I spent the next three hours looking for him, terrified as ever that this time I wouldn't find him. Abbi (aged just eight years old) used to tell me not to worry. "Lets face it Mum" she would say, "If anyone kidnaps him they'll pay us to take him back" which was probably true. However, I was always beside myself with anxiety until we found him and then I would be mad as hell with him as relief at finding him set in!

Following that incident, the headmistress advised me to try and get Luke statemented for his special educational needs that the school was struggling to meet, without allocated resources. In my total naivety I thought that it would be a relatively easy process. As I have detailed, it took a year, several reports, many letters, and our MP's and GP's help to even get the process off the ground and to begin to be taken seriously. I can't tell you, if you haven't been there, how lucky you are not to have been. I can't begin to tell you what it has been like to fight my boy at home and then to fight to get him help at school, knowing that his behaviour *is* his disability and yet to be the one on the receiving end of him and his anger. Even his dad had had enough at this point. He worked ever-longer hours and put in the occasional appearance at home and who can blame him? Only a mum would stay the distance. Your child is a part of you and I have always loved Luke intensely, even if I hate his behaviour, whilst understanding why he behaves that way and still wishing that I could give him away sometimes, often even, on a bad day!

He is highly intelligent, he is very aware of his differences without having the brain capacity yet to control them and is capable of achieving top marks in all subjects if his social inadequacies are addressed, not punished. (His attendance in year six was below 65% yet he achieved straight level 5's in his Sats.) The Government is beginning to recognise this and their recommendations for children on the autistic spectrum, given that it is a continuum, are spot on, but the implementation of those recommendations is still non-existent in our experience. Words are wonderful but actions speak much louder.

So back to that unforgettable summer holiday, before Luke started at senior school, when he was beside himself with fear and so was I, not knowing what we were meant to be doing or how to cope with him. Bearing in mind that a recognised trait of Aspergers Syndrome is a resistance to change, how where we supposed to cope with not even knowing for sure which school the LEA would choose for Luke to attend? I had even phoned Social Services in tears, begging them to help us, as he was so violent, aggressive and destructive. They came and did an assessment of us as a family, labelling Luke as a 'vulnerable child with a detachment disorder' and us as a family 'in need of help'. However, they then told us there were no resources available to offer us any help and our report 'remained on file'. The only help they did give us was three individual days at a special school for disabled children during the holidays. I then got a letter from them saying that they were closing our case! Just like that. Well thanks for nothing.

I am presently fighting the LEA again, this time for a specialist place for Luke in a school in Frome, the next county to ours, that specialises in educating children with Aspergers Syndrome. When I say fight, I mean that I have had to engage a solicitor to try and get my son a place in a school that caters for his level of disability. Legal aid is not available and so I have to fund the fight myself. This means that in a democratic country, governed by a socialist party, unless I have the money to fund my fight, my disabled son has no specialist educational rights to cater for his disability. He is expected to attend a mainstream school where he stands out like a sore thumb, in his eyes. He is taunted and laughed at, he has no skills to cope with the sheer size of the school, 1200 pupils, let alone the degree of self-management required of him, he is constantly misunderstood, has been taken out of class for inappropriate comments or behaviour and yet is expected to integrate without displaying any of the frustration which leads him to violent behaviour. He has been excluded for his disability and has been humiliated (by being taken out of class) for expressing an opinion which is considered politically incorrect. That's on the days that he actually *goes* to school.

It isn't the school's fault, Malmesbury School is an excellent mainstream school and they want to help Luke. I can't stress that enough. It is not the school's failing. Mrs. Higgs is head of the special needs department and she has bent over backwards to accommodate Luke, to help him achieve his potential, within the confines of available resources, and to understand his very particular personality. If it were down to her and her commitment he would succeed there. The school have tried so hard to educate Luke but how do you do that without understanding his needs, when they are complex and so different, all without a level of expertise and with that many different teachers coming and going? Luke is expected to fit in and the rules have to be maintained for the sake of the status quo. His logic is outside the norm and so he is living under such stress, trying to conform, having to constantly explain himself and often not succeeding, that he just can't cope.

What does all of this mean to Luke? What it means is that inclusion in mainstream school is for him social exclusion of the worst kind because it robs him of his self-esteem and it is not acceptable. Luke has tried to cope for two years at mainstream and he is failing. He is losing the motivation to succeed and I can't give up on him now. He can succeed and I am committed to making sure that he is at least given that chance.

Jan's tip: the first thing I would say is that you are your child's best hope if you are unlucky enough to be experiencing the same kind of problems that we have. I have been advised to make a total nuisance of myself at every level and I would if I could but I can't! It's a question of dignity.

Letters can't be ignored though, they have to be replied to and no matter how much you hate paperwork, try and keep records of all your phone calls, letters, incidents at school etc. if you possibly can because you have to produce hard evidence to back up your words.

At this very moment, as I write, I think that I should have tried harder to get Luke *specialist* help at the onset of mainstream school. I should have taken the LEA to a tribunal to challenge his statement once they had finally issued it. I wish I could rewrite the last two years for him and us. The trouble is that just living with Luke is totally exhausting, let alone fighting the system too.

The SEN helpline is 01 325 392 555 Website: www.sendist.gov.uk They are an independent tribunal set up by Act of Parliament for parents who cannot reach agreement with the LEA. They also consider parents' claims of disability discrimination in schools.

Communication is vital between you and your child's carer at school. Luke's teaching assistant, Claire Cork and I have had a daily diary system in which she tells me about his day at school, including any incidents that have occurred and I tell her of his perception of his day and any issues at home. However Luke has decided that he doesn't want that level of communication now that he is a teenager. He finds it degrading to carry a book between us which details his behaviour both at home and school and he has managed to 'lose' the latest diary. It has been extremely useful though, because Luke's version is exactly that and his perception is unusual sometimes, although it is very much his truth, so it has been vital to hear both sides of a story before making a judgment.

I don't want to frighten you but the change from primary school to secondary education is a big one for any child. If anxiety is an issue then it is essential that the transition be handled properly. The curriculum should come second to the child's need to familiarise with their new surroundings and once that particular anxiety has been addressed, then hopefully, the rest should follow. If it doesn't and you feel that it isn't working, act sooner rather than later because the present system is so unwieldy and takes forever.

Robert Love (www.langleywellington.co.uk) is a solicitor in Gloucester who specialises in education and I have just engaged him to challenge the LEA over their failure to provide Luke with the specialist education that his disability requires. It seems to be the only way.

Amazingly, this morning I have had a phone call from a charity called ASK, Advice and Services for Kids and young people and they have offered to help me fight the LEA, to come to meetings with me. They said that I won't have to fight by myself any more and I burst into tears of relief and amazement. (I had told God this morning at 6am that I had had enough and was at the end of my emotional tether. I hate fighting, my whole life is a fight sometimes)

I have just read that there is a book written by *Sandy Row*, published by *Jessica Kingsley* called *'Surviving the Special Educational Needs System: How to be a Velvet Bulldozer'* which sounds like the book I should have read three years ago.

Luke's tip: I find school so hard and it is because I know that I am different. There is a girl called Gemma in my form who has an extra something which makes her different (she has Down's Syndrome) and she looks different. I wish that I looked different too because I think that people are nicer to her than me. Most kids take the pee and call me names because they just don't get me. I hate being different and I am always being told off, just for being me. I so want to fit in and when I visited a school for other people like me I felt like I had found another home because they liked me as I am and didn't try and change me or make me think like them. They just accepted me for who I am. It is hard enough being a boy because boys are meant to be tough and strong and brave. I am all of those things but not in the same way as my friends. I can't play football but I can drive a go-kart brilliantly. Everyone says so. My skills are solitary and no one sees them at school. If you don't fit in and you don't know how to be part of a team and don't get the rules of boys and girls at this age, it is the loneliest place in the world. I am smart and I think that I am probably going to be a better adult than teenager but I still want to be accepted and I try really hard to get people to like me but I still want to be me at the same time. I really hope that I can survive but I wonder sometimes if I can. There are days when I can't be with anyone else because I can't stand trying to be the Luke that everyone says I have to be. Please can I just be me sometimes?

CHAPTER 16 THE END... OF LIFE AT THE EDGE

Life at **'The Edge'** came to an abrupt end. Paul and I were hardly communicating. He found it too difficult to compete with the level of attention that Luke demanded. Most men need to solve a problem and Luke is not solvable!

When Luke was diagnosed, I asked Paul to read the book by *Tony Attwood* on Aspergers Syndrome but he wouldn't or couldn't go there. He really didn't want to address the label of autism at all and that gave me nowhere to take it either. From then on we became more and more isolated within our marriage and Paul found ways to cope outside the home. Owning his own business meant that he always had valid reasons for not coming home. I felt very trapped inside the house, which was beginning to feel more like a prison and less like a home and I began to resent his level of freedom. My world had narrowed down to whether Luke could leave the house or not. I think Paul found it very hard to accept that his son wasn't the son he expected. Until that point there was always the hope that Luke would grow out of his behaviour and now we had to face reality of a different kind, a permanent kind. So he found safety in denial and often laid the blame for Luke's behaviour at my door, whilst I felt that if he were around more often then I would have more resources to cope. Resentment was building a Berlin wall between us and we had our own 'cold war' going on which was very chilly, to say the least.

No question that Paul loves Luke and he has a very good understanding of him in some ways, but he doesn't have the patience that Luke demands, who does? It's a funny thing, but as his mum I could get madder than mad with him, but woe betide anyone else who did. Because Paul and I are such different people with very different upbringings, morals and beliefs, our differences were highlighted by the way in which we would deal with Luke's behaviour. There was a middle ground but neither of us was willing or able to find it anymore. We weren't playing for the same team and so we were using Luke to get at each other. Every family mealtime (not that there were many of those) turned into a battle of wills. Luke's table manners leave a lot to be desired and Paul thought if he focused on those things that he felt he could do something about, at least he would be doing his parenting bit. Unfortunately, this just added to Luke's general anxiety and made him hate mealtimes even more. Every social gathering became an embarrassing one and Paul would be mad with Luke's behaviour whilst I would defend him because I understood what was driving him. It was becoming harder to keep up appearances and so we all but stopped socialising. Paul was at home rarely, preferring to stay away, so when he did come into the family and start telling Luke how to behave, we resented him. He had forfeited that right by his absences. To be fair to him, I don't know, given his personality, what he could have done to help because Luke's behaviour was such a nightmare, so he did the only thing that he knew worked for him and made himself scarce. I had a saying though 'when the going gets tough, Paul gets going' because that's how it felt to me. Luke, on the other hand, had mathematically worked out the day on which he would be strong enough to kill his father and written it down!

In the middle of this there was little Abbi. She was such a 'good' girl, always compliant, always well behaved. Almost non-existent at times. This worried me because she knew it was expected of her and also, it polarised her's and Luke's behaviour. He was always the 'troublesome one' and she was always the 'good one'. Those were their roles and they were stuck with them. I hated being typecast as a child and have always wanted to save my children that fate. So Luke got the blame for everything, rightly or wrongly and our little family wasn't working for any of us. Far worse though, it had a destruct button and I was about to push it.

Holidays were another nightmare as Luke couldn't sleep and couldn't adapt to the change of surroundings very easily. Consequently, I wanted to go back to somewhere familiar and Paul would need the challenge of a new place. We couldn't agree to compromise on anything and life at **'The Edge'** was just that. We had lived through so much and then EMI closed their Swindon offices (after their disastrous £80million record deal with Mariah Carey) and Paul's business failed as a direct result. He became more and more depressed and deeply angry too, with no business to escape to and no money coming in and Luke's behaviour to contend with. I am a talker and Paul isn't. We were locked in our own worlds of resentment and anger and something had to give. I hate arguments, confrontation, unhappiness and was living in an environment so alien to my nature that I could feel myself slipping into a hole which was deep and dark. I was scared that if I slipped too far down into that black place then I wouldn't be able to get out, ever. I began to have panic attacks when I was out shopping. My heart would race, my mouth go dry and metallic and I felt so sick, so faint that I was convinced I would die if I didn't get outside to the fresh air.

I reached a point where I couldn't cope with trying to make us all happy, broker yet another fragile peace amongst us, paper over the ever-widening cracks of family life, give everyone else their motivation and direction, keep smiling and thinking it would all work out in the end. *One day I just knew that I couldn't do it any longer.* Providing the energy for other people's happiness is just too much for anyone to sustain. For me it became a question of survival and if I didn't survive then neither would Luke and Abbi and it would all have been for nothing. I had a recurring nightmare that I died and no one would take Luke, no one wanted him because he was just too much trouble, which wasn't so far from the truth right then. I used to wake up crying, tears scalding my cheeks and my fear was so real that my heart started to race and I didn't know how to cope anymore. There was no way forward and no way back and we were all trapped in that hopeless waste of space called 'no-mans land'. It was a desolate place and I hope I never feel that lonely again. I used to wander the house without any motive or purpose, just the need to keep moving and a strange yearning to escape, to fly away and never come back.

Paul had been to the Philippines with his brother for eight days to escape from us over half-term and brought me back a Gucci purse, a real one! It seemed such a strange gesture, given our hostility towards each other and I felt as empty as the purse. I knew then that there was no going back and so, after 18 years of marriage, I told Paul that it was over for us. We were both so unhappy and lonely and this was the most honest conversation we had had in years. Looking back though, the irony of it was that I was the one who had been determined that we would survive, that we would beat the odds, that our children would never know the reality of a broken home. Yet I was the one who broke it all up.

We sold **'The Edge'** very quickly, once the decision was made to sell. It was a lovely house set in a third of an acre of land and it was *our* house that we had built from scratch, but it had long since stopped being a home. I had three weeks in which to find a new house to live in and the children and I moved into a small, terraced three-bedroom house in Malmesbury with a garden the size of a postage stamp and my friend Aura gave me a sign with the word 'Shalom' on which hangs in our hallway. *Peace.* How I longed for it. When we left our village we left behind all the security and familiarity that the children had ever known, including my parents who had moved there from our family home in Bristol.

Luke went shopping by himself recently for the first time, a big milestone for him and totally unexpectedly, he brought back a pair of earrings as a present for me! They are pretty, little delicate turquoise stones and I am wearing them now as I write. He bought them for me as a symbol of his love and gratefulness and understanding of what it costs me to be his mum and they are very precious. He told me in a carefully prepared little speech that I am selfless and that I am the best mum. The next minute I was the f***ing bitch again because I dared to say 'No' to his next request and he informed me that they only came from Argos anyway! Argos or not, they symbolise something very lovely for me; they are my symbol of hope. Not only that but they are something that I would have chosen for myself and that means that he *does* know me, he does know what I like and that is lovely beyond words.

And so we are surviving against the odds (which do seem to have been stacked against us) and right now we are standing at *The Edge* of another life, a new life, and we have hope again and hope brings with it the energy to face the future. So I will continue to fight for him, for his education, his happiness and his right to a future. To quote the L'Oreal advert in Luke's own inimitable way, 'Because I'm worth it' and he is.

ooooOoooo

EPILOGUE BEYOND LIFE AT THE EDGE

The story of life with Luke has been written in my head from his birth onwards and as each day unfolded, the weight of it grew until I longed to free up my mind and maybe, share some of the knowledge we had gained along the way. Somehow I knew that writing it down would help me make sense of all those moments that came flooding back, unbidden, at the most unexpected times. I was always taught as a child that I was capable of achieving something (even though my elder sister Fran was the brainy one and an impossible act to follow) and had always hoped that I could at least rise to the challenges life threw at me.

Well, loving and caring for my boy has been the toughest thing I have ever done. The physical and emotional costs have asked, no, *demanded* more of me than I could ever have imagined I was capable of giving, but beyond that by far is the fact that I love my children more than life and I would give anything in my power to make it a better space for them. So when I couldn't get Luke to eat the food I had prepared for him, or cuddle and comfort him when he had hurt himself or sometimes even touch him without him recoiling and running away from me, well that feels like a rejection of the most fundamental and nurturing place called motherhood. His level of frustration, even if you collect labels along the way to explain it, was displayed tangibly in the daily, sometimes hourly tantrums and I could do nothing to help him, to make it all better.

Paul took Luke and Abbi away for a week in the Easter holidays of 2005 and I knew then that it was probably the one and only chance I would get to write this book. There is no room for thinking, let alone writing, when Luke is around and so I used every available hour and time ceased to represent anything except a race to finish typing before they returned from their week away. Actually, the very last thing I wanted to do was spend precious 'Luke-free' time thinking, let alone writing, about Luke! I would very much have preferred to spend my time lying in the sun, toasting my body and enjoying the freedom and solitude right down to the tips of my toes but I couldn't just 'let go' of his lifetime's tension in a week's holiday. If I had allowed myself to relax I just knew I wouldn't be able to pick up where we'd left off, let alone where we would start again from. (Every time Luke leaves me, even if only to go to school, it always takes him a while to re-adjust and this had been a whole week. I was nervous and rightly so!)

It was so painful, re-living some of the memories, swollen with time and magnified with remembered hurts, that I sobbed as I wrote and once I had started, the words came tumbling out and I couldn't stop. (The difficult bit was cutting it down to size afterwards.) All that sadness for my child who is 'less than', yet so much 'more than' came flooding back. All the frustrations of his little lifetime, the illness which started it all, the ever present analysis of his behaviour and its' effect on each one of us, the perceived and imagined judgments of his hyperactivity and its' destructiveness, the (still ongoing) fight to get any kind of help, let alone specialist help, the sleepless nights and the utter bleakness of those lonely days when hope *was* an empty word and our reality stretched out before us like a menacing dark cloud. The happy times were incredibly precious though and we lived for those moments, storing up the imprint of laughter on our minds. Luke can be very funny, even when he is madder than mad, and sometimes we choose laughter as the best, the only way out.

Writing our story proved to be such a cathartic experience though and if no one ever reads this book, it will have been worth the effort. Just to relieve my brain of the memories and to remind myself that we really have packed more dramas into Luke's short life (although not by choice) than some people pack into a lifetime of reasoned choices, that made it more than worth the effort. However, besides that, everyone we meet these days seems to know someone on the autistic spectrum and so I am hoping that our story will have a valuable part to play in your life too. If you are fortunate enough to be reading this, then it means I have been successful in publishing it!

I also hope that Luke himself will have a chance to tell people what life is like for someone like him and by doing so, open up what is still very much a misunderstood and taboo subject in our make-believe world of air-brushed perfection, of skinny (role) models and 'famous for being famous' icons of nothingness. He has to work twice as hard as everyone else just to stand still, especially at school, and I think he deserves, as do all children like him, the understanding and respect from society of what it's like when you constantly have to rethink yourself, just to try and fit in.

Luke is now a strapping fifteen-year-old boy, in his first GSCE year. He is still at Malmesbury mainstream school (despite our fight with the LEA for specialist education) and he has taught them so much about autism and ADHD, in many ways he has had to re-educate the education system.

There are still very few days when I don't have to speak to his school and deal with an incident, a misunderstanding or an issue that either they or Luke don't understand. Only this morning I took Abbi in after a physiotherapist appointment to discover Luke in reception with a pained look of frustration and anger on his pale face after yet another incident, this time between him and a teacher in the library. He isn't quiet enough for the library, (you remember he only talks loud or louder) but he wanted to go there to meet up with a few of his friends. Most teachers assume that he is being loud deliberately and as you now know, he's not. So yet again, I found myself trying to rescue Luke from himself and he hates that, finds it unjust and unfair to be isolated and held responsible for what is actually a part of his disability, and at his age who wants their mum doing the talking for them? The trouble with some teachers is that they aren't in the business of being taught, they only like to teach and those are usually the ones Luke falls foul of.

He comes now with a broken home behind him, with all the bewilderment that brings to any child, let alone an autistic one. And yet he is succeeding beyond our wildest dreams for him. He is intelligent, funny, polite in adult company, (well sometimes!) still a brilliant mimic and he can laugh at himself before someone else does. More than that again, he is so articulate in explaining himself in a way that is extraordinary for someone of his age, let alone someone with his labels, bearing in mind that Aspergers Syndrome is, first and foremost, a communication disorder. I had a telephone conversation this morning with a professional who met Luke last week in the course of her work and she said that she was amazed at his poise, confidence and maturity! (I had to check that my ears were working correctly, I am still not used to people paying me compliments about my son.)

He still hates going to school and we still have a fight to get him there most days but he works harder than hard to re-programme that inflexible part of his brain that is change-resistant and each day at the moment is a stepping stone to a better tomorrow. He now tries lots of different foods and his diet is significantly better. He also hugs me and kisses me often, spontaneously and without any obvious teenage embarrassment. This place we inhabit now has been so worth waiting for, it is better than I ever imagined and yet we still never dare to take anything for granted. How can we? His condition is a lifelong one and anxiety can and often does tip the scales of what is still a very delicate balance.

Our story has turned the corner of hope though and we have many more good days than bad. We no longer live with a frustrated and violent Luke but a sociable, mostly happy and healthy Luke who is still loud and larger than life. He has a massive amount of energy, which still hits you full on, and *most* of the time now he has the emotions of a teenager in a teenager's body with the intellect of a teenager, which is just as it should be. Luke is still Luke though and he remains just as unpredictable, but at this place in time he is no longer out of control and that pleases him more than he can say.

The photo on the front cover was taken on 28th January 2006. A lovely, completely spontaneous (and back then, still relatively rare) moment between Luke and I, captured on camera by my friend Anna at my wedding to the loveliest man on God's green earth. When my marriage to Paul ended, he threw at me (in one of our more bitter exchanges) the stark reality that I would never again be part of a couple. Who would be prepared to take me on board with Luke in tow? Well, in my experience, God often thinks 'outside the box' that we like to keep Him in and I now have a gorgeous new husband who loves me enough to have welcomed the three of us into his life. (That is another story in itself.)

Luke and Abbi have lived for most of the past year in a four-bedroom house, as part of an extended family with four stepbrothers, not enough room to swing our cat Kibbi and so many changes that familiar has become an unfamiliar word. We, in return and putting it mildly, have given the new males in our lives a more interesting space to inhabit! I like to think that as a result of our input they would all say they have a better informed, hands-on understanding of life in general and a much greater appreciation of the differences that make us all individuals, whilst acquiring patience by the bucket load. (Talking of patience, phoning a certain mobile phone company, going through about 100 options and the most annoying background music ever, only to get cut off when you do finally, actually get to speak to a real-life person, that's the patience lesson I could do without! It doesn't exactly recommend their business either, does it?)

Luke has risen to the challenges of our new life with his own particular style of resisting each and every step of the way. He has developed new relationships and learnt the hard way to love his new family and them, him! And very especially, he has learnt to love and respect me in a way that I would never once have dared hope for. (He is still of the opinion though, that women are only born to serve men and wouldn't some men love that, if the truth were told!) His dad lives in Bristol and Luke sees him most weekends and really enjoys the change (!) of scenery, adapting incredibly well from country to city life - something I'm sure he would never have been able to cope with if we had always pandered to his strong demand for sameness - and they now have a very good relationship. Funnily enough, Luke has a new obsession and one that I would *never* have predicted - clothes - and he has, in his own words, become 'a fashion victim' who dresses for the occasion. His wardrobe now holds several suits and he loves the sense of identity that the 'uniform' of a businessman affords him.

This year (2006) he went shopping in early December, again by himself and this time he went to the *'Swarovski'* shop and bought me a beautiful crystal necklace which he placed in a pink box filled with my favourite sweets, all wrapped up with a matching ribbon. He gave it to me at Christmas with a kiss and his love. Later on, after I had dried my tears, (this time happy ones!) he asked me if the lady that had served him would have been more or less impressed if he had told her he was buying the present for a girlfriend rather than his mum. He still has to weigh up every situation and figure out what is the best possible outcome for him because none of it comes naturally.

And so, as before, we will continue to fight for him, for his education and his right to be accepted for who he is, how he is, as himself, as Luke with all his labels. He is an amazing boy and I hope I have done him justice without betraying too much of his privacy. Thank you for reading our story.

ooooOoooo